# Tackling Regional Disparities in Europe Through Growth

*Young Liberal Perspectives*

## AUTHORS

Igor Caldeira (coordinator), Aleko Stoyanov, Alexander Hammond, Ashmita Krishna, Daniel Hinst, Egija Gailuma, Felix Gießmann, Felix Reimann, Jelena Jesajana, Justyna Michalik, Keith Henry, Manel Msalmi, Maximilian Heilmann, Sid Lukkassen, Toine Schouteten

**Cover design**: Edgaras Mascinkas

**Copy/proof-reader**: Harriet Ainscough

*Published by the European Liberal Forum asbl with the support of LYMEC. Co-funded by the European Parliament. Neither the European Parliament nor the European Liberal Forum asbl (nor LYMEC) are responsible for the content of this publication, or for any use that may be made of it. The views expressed herein are those of the author(s) alone. These views do not necessarily reflect those of the European Parliament, the European Liberal Forum asbl (and LYMEC).*

© 2015 European Liberal Forum
First Printing: 2015

ISBN 978-1-326-27492-4

ELF – European Liberal Forum, asbl
Brussels, Belgium
www.liberalforum.eu

LYMEC – European Liberal Youth , asbl
Brussels, Belgium
www.lymec.eu

## Contents

**ABOUT THE AUTHORS** .................................................vii

**Foreword** by **Felicita Medved**, President of the European Liberal Forum ................................................xi

**Foreword** by **Andreja Potočnik**, ALDE Group member, Committee of the Regions ............................................xiii

**Introduction** by **Vedrana Gujic**, President of LYMEC, the European Liberal Youth............................................15

**ALEKO STOYANOV** - Regional Disparities in Europe – The Case of Bulgaria ....................................................17

**ALEXANDER HAMMOND** - Regional Disparities: Facts, Problems and Solutions ...............................................23

**ASHMITA KRISHNA** - Regional Disparities and the Individual Member States... We Need a Liberal Approach..33

**DANIEL HINŠT** - Getting Back to Growth: Clues for Europe in a Global Economy .........................................37

**EGIJA GAILUMA** - Getting Back to Growth: Clues for Europe in a Global Economy .........................................41

**FELIX GIEßMANN** - Challenges and Opportunities of the EU Energy and Resource Efficiency Policy .................51

**FELIX REIMANN** - European Financial Accounting as a Factor for Transparency and Economic Growth ...............55

**IGOR CALDEIRA** - Why Portuguese Municipalities Fail: breaking vicious circles to promote growth.....................61

**JELENA JESAJANA** - Regional Disparities: The case of Latgale ...................................................................73

**JUSTYNA MICHALIK** - Regional disparities: Poland in Europe, Poland vs. Europe ..............................................**79**

**KEITH HENRY** - Using Agenda 21 to Address Regional Disparities ...............................................................**85**

**MANEL MSALMI** - Partnership Agreements and Trade and Growth in World Affairs, the Key Solution to a Healthy European Economy .....................................................**93**

**MAXIMILIAN HEILMANN** - European Future: Cooperation and collaboration for a growing European economy............................................................**97**

**SID LUKKASSEN** - Europe: A Path Towards All Your Innovative Needs.....................................................**101**

**TOINE SCHOUTETEN** - Opening up the Union: the Increase of EU-Connectivity by Railroad .....................**127**

# ABOUT THE AUTHORS

**ALEKO STOYANOV** is an individual member of LYMEC. He studied European Studies at the University of National and World Economy, Sofia and International Relations at Bonn University. Currently he is finishing his Masters degree in Political Science at the Central European University, Budapest.

**ALEXANDER HAMMOND** is a trilingual British law student currently at Reading University and an active member of the Liberal Democrat Party in the UK. He has lived in Hong Kong and the Netherlands as well as the UK, and has a great interest in European affairs.

**ASHMITA KRISHNA** is Dutch. She has been an Individual Member of LYMEC since 2014 and an Associate Member of the ALDE Party (#1000), alongside having been a member of the JOVD (Netherlands, LYMEC member) since 2008.

**DANIEL HINŠT** is a member, and former international officer, of the Croatian MHNS. Daniel is a president of the Centre for Public Policy and Economic Analysis, a Croatian free market think-tank. His key areas of policy research and advocacy are the EU single market liberalization, TTIP and CETA, market deregulation and tax reform.

**EGIJA GAILUMA** comes from Riga, Latvia. She holds a Bachelor's degree of applied sciences in Economics and Business from the Stockholm School of Economics in Riga. She has been involved in politics since 2010 and is currently a member of the liberal party *For development of Latvia* (Latvijas Attistibai, Latvia). She has participated and contributed to several youth leadership projects that are aimed at cooperation between the EU and other countries.

**FELIX GIEßMANN** is from the German City Wuppertal. He has been a member of the Young Liberals since 2009 and is an Associate Member of the ALDE Party. Felix is 21 years old and studies Political Science and Economics. He works as a secretary and networker for political affairs in the "Innovation Centre Northrhine-Westfalia (Innovationszentrum NRW e.V.)".

**FELIX REIMANN** was born in Germany in 1992. He has been a member of JuLis since 2012 and the treasurer of the JuLis Berlin since 2015. Currently, he is studying Industrial Engineering at the Berlin Institute of Technology and will start his master courses this fall. His interests include financial markets and the impact of EU policies on financial reporting. He currently lives in Berlin, Germany.

**IGOR CALDEIRA** is Portuguese. He is an Individual Member of LYMEC, Associate Member of the ALDE Party, as well as a member of Jeunes MR (Belgium, LYMEC member) and MLS (Portugal, ELF member). He was a delegate for the Individual Members' Section (2010-2012), Board member of LYMEC (2012-2014) and is the Secretary General of LYMEC for the mandate of 2014-2016. He studied Political Science and Philosophy in Portugal and Belgium.

**JELENA JESAJANA** is from Riga, Latvia. She has been an Individual Member of LYMEC since 2011 and an Associate Member of the ALDE Party. Last year she also joined Latvijas Attistibai (Latvia, ALDE member). Jelena was a delegate for the Individual Members' Section (2012-2013), and is currently a Board member of LYMEC responsible for political campaigns and IMS section.

**JUSTYNA MICHALIK** is an Individual Member of LYMEC. She studied at Jagiellonian University in Cracow and has a Masters in International Relations and European Studies and a Bachelors in International Cultural Studies. She has been awarded international scholarships at the University of Vienna and "St.

Kliment Ohridski", University of Sofia. In 2013 she was a trainee in the European Parliament Information Office in Warsaw.

**KEITH HENRY** is the first International Officer of Ógra Fianna Fáil the youth wing of Ireland's largest party at local government. Prior to this Keith served as National Chairman from 2012-2015 and as regional organiser for his native North West region from 2009-2011. Keith also formed part of the delegation which brought Ógra into LYMEC as full members in 2014.

**MANEL MSALMI** is Belgian-Tunisian.She is a communication advisor for the Young liberals in Brussels (Jeunes MR), has been a member of the Francophone liberal party in Belgium(MR) since 2010 and an associate member of Alde Party since 2014.She has also been a member of Jeunes Mr since 2012 and a committee member of the Liberal trade union of Education in Belgium since 2012 (SLFP Enseignement).

**MAXIMILIAN HEILMANN** is German. He has been a Member of JuLis since 2008 and is active in the International Committee of the youth organization of the federal liberal party in Germany. He is a scholarship holder of the Friedrich-Naumann Foundation and studies Business Administration and Engineering with a minor in Education along with his exchange programs in the United Stated, Latvia and in Gießen.

**SID LUKKASSEN** (1987) has a MA in history, philosophy, and is currently a Ph.D candidate. He is a city councillor for the VVD in Duiven, the Netherlands, and author of the recently published book *Avondland en Identiteit* (Occident and Identity).

**TOINE SCHOUTETEN** lives in Amsterdam, the Netherlands. He has been a member of the International Secretariat of the JOVD since 2012 and is a member of the LYMEC Working Group on Comparative Liberal Politics. Next to this, Toine is active within the Amsterdam department of the VVD and is an individual member of ALDE.

# Foreword by Felicita Medved, President of the European Liberal Forum

From the beginning of the process of European integration, and particularly with each subsequent enlargement, disparities of different kinds have existed between the European regions and the EU Member States. In the sustained period of economic growth in the EU Economy, and as a result of the European Regional or Cohesion policy, disparities between regions were narrowing, but since the crisis of 2008 these positive trends have changed. While the economic and social effects of the economic crisis, such as high rates of unemployment, have hit almost all parts of the EU, the territorial impact on European regions and cities has been mixed. In a number of less developed Member States and regions developments appear not to be going in the right direction and even in many cities in the more developed Member States levels of poverty and exclusion have increased. These worrying developments mean that the targets of the Europe 2020 strategy on smart, inclusive and sustainable growth are now significantly further away than when they were first set.

Tasked with a very wide and ambitious mandate of promoting Liberalism, liberal ideas and policies and of contributing to the democratic development of the European public sphere, the European Liberal Forum (ELF) has concentrated its resources on a few focus areas. Liberal solutions for the European economy, promotion of the rule of law and the future of the EU, as well as capacity building to strengthen the European liberal dimension, are high on the agenda of our political foundation. Diversity of our membership, consisting of a number of European think tanks, political foundations and institutions and partnership with the ALDE Party and the European Liberal Youth (LYMEC) enables us to promote active citizenship, particularly with regard to young Europeans. It also provides for an exchange of knowledge to the reflection and debate among liberals and so, to increase our capacity of action at the European, national, regional and local levels.

One of the core aspects of our work consists in issuing publications on Liberalism and European public policy issues. The publication you are about to read presents young liberal perspectives on 'Tackling regional disparities in the EU.' It is the outcome of the seminar gathering of committed young liberals from across Europe in Warsaw in March 2015. There they presented and discussed their opinions about different levels of development across European regions and exchanged views on how to tackle regional disparities by promoting growth based on innovation, private investment and trade.

Within the context of the EU's main investment policy, comprising almost a third of the total EU budget, and its links to Europe 2020 and yearly cycle of economic policy coordination of structural reform processes linked to the European Semester, the views of young liberals that not only look at the underlying dynamics of regions but call for action are worth exploring.

Within the efforts of the ELF to help the renewal of ever new generations of young liberals, this contribution of LYMEC, the European Liberal Youth, to the ELF's publication series shows, once again, that investment in youth proves to be the future of the EU and the key of reversing the trend of growing regional disparities, particularly when linked to the ways of improving and increasing their democratic participation in political decisions.

# Foreword by Andreja Potočnik, ALDE Group member, Committee of the Regions

Since 2009 the term "economic crisis" seems to have cemented its place in our daily vocabulary and tackling the deepest recession of the post-WWII era came to the forefront of the policy agendas of all EU-Member states. Six years later and the European Union is being challenged by regional disparities.

The economic future is uncertain, and more so for the newer Member States, with the good news being that the EU has multiple mechanisms in place to facilitate growth and economic development (ERDF, ESF, The Cohesion Fund, EUSF and IPA).

To paraphrase the famous words of an even more famous person, let's not ask what the EU can do for us, but remember the key role the national and regional governments need to play in promoting structural reforms, exercising fiscal responsibility, boosting job-creating investments and economic growth. All Member States, in particular those with more limited fiscal space, must ensure efficient use of resources, prioritize investment- and growth-related expenditure in their budgets and best utilise the EU mechanisms at their disposal. Regional policies that are already bearing fruit need to keep their course.

Every crisis also brings with it new opportunities. The arrival of a new Commission gave us the opportunity for a fresh start and the tools to overcome regional disparities are in our hands. Let us best use them!

# Introduction by Vedrana Gujic, President of LYMEC, the European Liberal Youth

LYMEC, as the umbrella organisation of liberal youth in Europe, shares the ongoing common concern of young people in Europe – the state of our economy and its reflection on our future growth, jobs and lives.

The economic crisis left large parts of Europe with high unemployment rates, slowdown of economic growth and depopulation. The areas which were poorly developed were even more isolated, leading to evident regional disparities and economic and demographic cleavages between different parts of the Union.

As liberals, we want to see a growth oriented, open and competitive Europe that invests in research and innovation, new technologies, education and boosts job creation. We want a Europe that builds its economic growth on the foundations that were laid in the four freedoms, completing its Single Market in all of its aspects and enabling regional development through free trade of all of its goods and services.

Following the liberal visions of Europe, LYMEC gathered a group of young authors to discuss the topic of the evident regional imbalances and give us their solutions leading to growth and jobs in every corner of the European Union.

# ALEKO STOYANOV
# - Regional Disparities in Europe – The Case of Bulgaria

The motto of the EU, "United in diversity" which was officially introduced in the year 2000 mainly to signify, "...how Europeans have come together ... to work for peace and prosperity, ... being enriched by the continent's many different cultures, traditions and languages"[1] has been reflected to a great extent in another field of the EU – its regional policy.

The European regional policy, the origins of which can be traced back to the 50's with the signing of the Treaties of Rome in 1957[2] has undergone different transformations in order to adapt itself to the ever-increasing challenges of its time. Initiated as a tool aiming to, "... reduce structural disparities between EU regions, foster balanced development throughout the EU and promote real equal opportunities for all..."[3], based on the concepts of solidarity and economic and social cohesion, the EU regional policy continues to serve its purposes. Today the EU regional policy amounts to some €347 billion - almost one third of the whole EU budget[4] and through its different objectives supports more than 200 regions in all 28 EU member states.

---

[1] Europa, How the EU works, the EU motto, http://europa.eu/about-eu/basic-information/symbols/motto/index_en.htm

[2] In the preamble of the Treaty of Rome is stipulated that one of the aims is "reducing the differences existing between the various regions and the backwardness of the less favoured regions"

[3] Europa, Summaries of EU legislation, Regional policy, History of the policy, retrieved from:
http://europa.eu/legislation_summaries/regional_policy/index_en.htm

[4] European Commission, Regional Policy, retrieved from:
http://ec.europa.eu/regional_policy/index.cfm/en/policy/what/history/

Bulgaria, which joined the EU in 2007, had the opportunity to benefit from the EU's regional policy instruments such as the European Regional and Development Fund, the Cohesion Fund, the European Social Fund and even the EU Solidarity Fund. However, seven years later 5 out of all 6 Bulgarian regions are still among the poorest in the EU. This fact raises a question - what are the challenges that Bulgaria faces in catching up with the more developed regions and what could be done to close this gap?

**Challenges**

The territory of Bulgaria is divided into 6 planning regions – the Northwest, North-Central, Northeast, Southeast, South-Central and Southwest regions. Yet, these regions cannot be regarded fully as such. The reason is that they are not administrative-territorial entities but rather statistical units that were established to correspond to the Nomenclature of Territorial Units for Statistics – NUTS. In addition, in the case of Bulgaria, the local municipalities are the main actors responsible for the implementation of the regional policy. However, they vary greatly from one another, which hampers the possibility of pursuing a coherent and well-coordinated policy.

Moreover, the leading role of the municipalities causes additional problems. The size of the municipality directly affects its capacity to absorb EU funds. The major municipalities have the expertise to prepare their applications, secure grants and implement their projects while the smaller municipalities are usually understaffed and lacking know-how. This, in practice, cuts the access of the latter to the financial instruments of the EU. Hence, the bulk of the financial resources go to the larger municipalities, a process which further deepens the disparity at national and European level. For instance, the capital Sofia (which is situated in the South-West region) is attracting a considerable part of the human resources and foreign investments, thus depriving other regions of their human capital and specialists. If we add the emigration flows to the equation the picture is even gloomier for the rest of the country.

Last but not least there is one more problem that can be outlined which is related to the fiscal concentration. The bigger part of the money in the municipality budgets comes from the state budget in contrast to most of the other European countries where the amount of funds allocated through the regional and municipal budgets is almost as equal to that coming from the central budget.[5] In 2014 the cabinet has transferred 2.385 billion. leva to the municipalities, around €1.2 billion[6], which amounts to almost 3% of the country's GDP[7] (in comparison the budget for defence is almost 1 billion leva or around €500 million and for health is circa 400 million leva or around €200 million)[8]. To some extent this issue could be tackled with credits of the Fund for Local Authorities and Governments (FLAG). However, the credits need to be paid back with money that, again, will come from the municipality budgets.

In addition, the centralization of the regional policy and the approach of the government to distribute a certain amount of money to each municipality does not allow for coherent investments. For instance, during the previous programme period many small and middle-sized Bulgarian cities used the regional policy funds to renovate their main squares. It is not a crime to improve the city gardens and its surroundings, thus making it

---

[5] Prof. Dr. Hadjinikolov Dimitar. "The European Funds and the Regional Cohesion – the Case of Bulgaria", Round Table: EU Funds – National Effective? Partnership Agreement Bulgaria – EC 2014-2020, Hilton Hotel, Sofia, 11 October 2013, Conference Presentation.

[6] Ministry of Finance of the Republic of Bulgaria, National Budget 2014, retrieved from: http://www.minfin.bg/bg/page/850

[7] National Statistical Institute of Bulgaria, GDP 2014, retrieved from: http://www.nsi.bg/bg/content/2206/%D0%B1%D0%B2%D0%BF-%D0%BF%D1%80%D0%BE%D0%B8%D0%B7%D0%B2%D0%BE%D0%B4%D1%81%D1%82%D0%B2%D0%B5%D0%BD-%D0%BC%D0%B5%D1%82%D0%BE%D0%B4-%D0%BD%D0%B0%D1%86%D0%B8%D0%BE%D0%BD%D0%B0%D0%BB%D0%BD%D0%BE-%D0%BD%D0%B8%D0%B2%D0%BE

[8] Ministry of Finance of the Republic of Bulgaria, National Budget 2014, retrieved from: http://www.minfin.bg/bg/page/850

more pleasant for the citizens, however such fund absorbing does not only not lead to economic growth but just the opposite, it requires additional costs for maintenance.[9]

**Solutions**

As presented above there are many obstacles that hinder the cohesion processes in Bulgaria. Nonetheless, there are several measures that could be undertaken in order to improve the situation and mitigate the negative impacts caused by the shortcomings of the regional policy implementation in the country.

In the first place, a stronger cooperation between the structures working at local and national level should be established. For instance, this could be achieved by developing partnerships between the local NGOs and associations working at a regional level, which could also be supported by the central government. In this way a more coherent bottom up – top down approach could be applied. In addition, there public-private partnerships could be created with the local businesses that could boost the regional economy.

Secondly, there is a need for better geographical balance. As mentioned earlier, very often the bulk of the EU funds go to several large municipalities such as Sofia-city, Plovdiv, Burgas etc. A possible solution could be restructuring the six planning regions into administrative ones. Also, the capital Sofia could become a separate region. Keeping in mind that this is the most populated and developed region in Bulgaria its differentiation would lead to an increase in the allocated funds for the rest of the South-West region, which would allow the latter to catch up with the more developed regions in Europe. Another answer to the regional problems could be the reduction of the number of municipalities and especially of those that are not economically vital. In such a

---

[9] Georgiev, O.: "Bulgaria na tri skorosti", Capital, 20 March 2015: http://www.capital.bg/politika_i_ikonomika/bulgaria/2015/03/20/2496147_bulga riia_na_tri_skorosti/?sp=1#storystart

way a step towards a moderate polycentrism rather than the current radical mono-centrism model could be made.

Thirdly, there is a need for a greater socio-economic effect. Instead of measuring the amount of the absorbed funds and the number of the implemented projects it would be better to evaluate how they have affected the socio-economic development in the respected region(s). As mentioned earlier the improvement of city squares will not generate growth and attract investment itself.

Last but not least, the strengthening of the civic element in the process of determining the regional priorities could lead to a clearer identification of the most acute problems and to a deeper understanding how they could be addressed better.

## Conclusion

Since its establishment more than 50 years ago the EU regional policy has developed significantly. Today the EU has allocated around one-third of its budget to fight its regional disparities. However, as exemplified in the case of Bulgaria, there are still many obstacles – administrative division, size and capacity of the municipalities to absorb funds, too much financial dependency on the central government, funding unprofitable projects and investing in municipalities which are not financially viable that need to be overcome until this goal is reached. Nevertheless, there are also some policies and measures that the Bulgarian authorities could implement - better administrative structuring, improving the cooperation between non-government sector, business and public authorities, investment in profitable projects that facilitate an economic growth which, if applied properly, could lead to a higher integration and bring the Bulgarian regions closer to the more developed ones.

**Sources**:

- Europa, How the EU works, the EU motto, http://europa.eu/about-eu/basic-information/symbols/motto/index_en.htm
- Europa, Summaries of EU legislation, Regional policy, History of the policy, http://europa.eu/legislation_summaries/regional_policy/index_en.htm
- European Commission, Regional Policy, http://ec.europa.eu/regional_policy/index.cfm/en/policy/what/history/
- Georgiev, O.: "Bulgaria na tri skorosti", Capital, 20 March 2015, http://www.capital.bg/politika_i_ikonomika/bulgaria/2015/03/20/2496147_bulgariia_na_tri_skorosti/?sp=1#storystart
- Ministry of Finance of the Republic of Bulgaria, National Budget 2014: http://www.minfin.bg/bg/page/850
- National Statistical Institute of Bulgaria, GDP 2014, http://www.nsi.bg/bg/content/2206/%D0%B1%D0%B2%D0%BF-%D0%BF%D1%80%D0%BE%D0%B8%D0%B7%D0%B2%D0%BE%D0%B4%D1%81%D1%82%D0%B2%D0%B5%D0%BD-%D0%BC%D0%B5%D1%82%D0%BE%D0%B4-%D0%BD%D0%B0%D1%86%D0%B8%D0%BE%D0%BD%D0%B0%D0%BB%D0%BD%D0%BE-%D0%BD%D0%B8%D0%B2%D0%BE
- Prof. Dr. Hadjinikolov Dimitar. "The European Funds and the Regional Cohesion – the Case of Bulgaria", Round Table: EU Funds – National Effective? Partnership Agreement Bulgaria – EC 2014-2020, Hilton Hotel, Sofia, 11 October 2013, Conference Presentation.

# ALEXANDER HAMMOND - Regional Disparities: Facts, Problems and Solutions

There are many issues associated with the regional discrepancies of the EU. Many are a hindrance to development and progress, whilst some allow for exploitation of characteristics of particular regions, for their lower wages or perhaps lower taxes. However, the majority view is that within a single market it is ideal to have as little divergence as possible in order to encourage a more unified economy and therefore more stability[10].

Approximately 18% of the community represents around half the wealth and half the research and technological capabilities in the EU, and this is clearly not desirable for a stable and strong economy. The unemployment rates vary from below 5% to over 25%, the GDP per capita varies from approximately 6000 euros to 83,500 euros and the difference in debt between states is between around 180% of GDP to 8% of GDP, all within the EU[11].

There are huge differences in infrastructure, business opportunities, efficiency of the economy and access to technology, and this has a negative effect on the EU as a whole, as other states must provide more to help states that may have barely made it into the EU due to their flagging economies.

This paper will attempt to address some of these issues and provide general commentary and solutions to them, focussing on the areas of de-industrialisation and unemployment, the financial disparities, technology, corruption, which arguably has become a

---

[10] "Optimal Integration in the Single Market: A Synoptic Review"; Europe Economics; April 2013

[11] The Data Team; "Taking Europe's pulse"; The Economist; Feb 13th 2015

problem as big as any the EU has faced, and the need for changes within the mechanisms of the EU to allow for these disparities to disappear.

The de-industrialisation of Europe during the late 1970s to the present day is one of the main reasons for disparity of wealth in the EU, in part due to the advent of advanced technology, and the shift it caused in creating more tertiary sector jobs. With the emergence of large industrial economies in Asia and South America, the EU must focus on the areas in which it is more competent and not attempt to compete in the same way. Whilst secondary sector industries continue to thrive across the EU, in Germany and Italy for example, manufacturing specialised, high-quality and technologically advanced goods, the infrastructure that exists for producing other goods lies unused, or it is only certain areas of a state, such as northern Italy, really have the state's secondary industry[12].

After the fall of the USSR countries within its influence suffered blunt and sudden de-industrialisation, as unprofitable enterprises failed when introduced to a free market system, leaving a huge gap in the economy. It is no surprise, therefore, that member states that have industries that have been undermined by foreign competitors have some of the highest unemployment rates in the EU[13]. Deindustrialisation across the EU hasn't all been disastrous; one very good example can be found in Germany. Germany underwent some deindustrialisation after the Second World War and again after reunification. However, not only does Germany have a thriving secondary industry sector, it also has the highest GDP of any EU state[14]. This is due to the fact that the industry not only survived, but became more specialised and high-tech, and for those areas of industry that didn't survive, especially in eastern Germany, there was a tertiary industry boom that created more

---

[12] "The Socioeconomic Diversity of European Regions" "" (ibid.)
13 Oleh Havrylyshyn; "Fifteen Years of Transformation in the Post-Communist World"; (9 November 2007).
14 The Data Team; "Taking Europe's pulse"; The Economist; Feb 13th 2015

jobs and means today Germany has the second lowest unemployment rates in the EU.

However, when tackling regional disparity, it is important to remember that many states are not as fortunate in circumstances as Germany. Greece has the highest unemployment level of any EU member state, at over 25%. Greece has suffered deindustrialisation, not purely by secondary areas turning over to tertiary industries, but simply that the secondary industries were no longer viable and ceased to operate, leaving a stranded workforce that did not have the skills required to interface with a service and technology based economy that is becoming the norm amongst European states[15]. A similar sort of sudden shock decrease has happened elsewhere, such as Poland, and highlights the drastic need for growth in the tertiary sectors of these states' economies in order to reduce the regional disparities in wealth, unemployment and growth.

This is where the Europe 2020 strategy is vital, as it encourages and creates a framework for improving education in the EU and integrating technology into the economy in a more profound way to create service and technology based employment. Such goals include but are not limited to; creating a Digital Single Market, boosting internet trust and security, guaranteeing the provision of much faster internet access, encouraging investment in research and innovation and enhancing digital literacy, skills and inclusion[16] . These are commendable goals, ones that should encourage the creation of jobs and more efficiency in business; so that a company in Poland can more easily deal with a firm in Portugal for example, through the Digital Single Market and by being more closely integrated with technology in their business models. However, it is disappointing not to find a concrete goal for consistent internet coverage in the EU; although it is commended as a good indicator

---

15 World Economic Outlook Database, April 2013 edition
[16] John G. Chilas; "Overall economic performance of Greece and the deindustrialization thesis"; Journal of Statistics and Management Systems, Volume 6, Issue 3; 2003

and goal in the Europe 2020 strategy it is still being left down to the private sector too much to get people online; EU subsidies for families and businesses to get access should be increased and subsidies should not go to the companies that provide internet coverage. It would be fairly easy for most if not all of Europe to have competent internet coverage, but it is not touched upon, which is perturbing, as universal internet coverage would close the gap in disparities between regions incredibly quickly in today's world, with online banking services and business conducted online, it would speed up the growth and development of less advanced areas in the EU and allow for cultural and social cohesion as well as better education and understanding and use of the EU's mechanisms.

Education is high on the agenda for Europe 2020 and the focus on the knowledge economy and technology aiding business should be taken into account when talking about education. States with the correct education programs and initiatives can create a generation of skilled labourers that don't have to compete with multiple competitor markets outside the EU, with perhaps the exception of the USA and Japan, because they can be so specialised and advanced in their fields that they can be part of a new wave of revival in the EU's most under-developed and lagging economies in the tertiary and quaternary sectors, and revive industry in economies with the infrastructure for it by providing the necessary tools for the private sector to begin producing high-tech and luxury goods that not only outdo foreign market competitors, but circumvent them too. Technology is one of the most important parts of life in this age, and the EU must embrace it in order to allow wealth to be created in less economically developed areas.

Besides the necessary technological advancement in the EU to ensure more harmonious and homogenous economies in the regions, the financial sector will play an important role and the market itself will have to change to reduce regional differences. The EU many that are behind in terms of development and wealth, the EU's proficiency in banking and finance could be used as a catalyst for promoting growth and bringing them on-board with schemes of knowledge sharing. The EU has the potential to become the world's financial hub, with many different states bringing their own skills and resources to the table, and allowing for regions that perhaps have not had the chances to grow such sectors, to converge towards a similar level and status. It would also allow for businesses in the EU to be granted loans more easily by levelling the playing field in terms of financial capabilities and resources of member states and accelerate the growth of regional economies and businesses and therefore make them more competitive and viable overall. At the moment it is difficult for businesses, especially small ones, to get the funding and investment they need to be successful[17], and so a greater ability to allow for this throughout Europe would be a boon to the entire region's economy and result in growth in less developed regions, shrinking the gap in wealth throughout the EU and strengthening the internal market.

Besides this, the convergence of European banking into a practically continent-wide banking and financial hub would allow for massive bargaining power with markets and states outside the EU; the world would come to Europe for its financial needs. Just as China has a great position around the negotiating table due to its cheap export capacity and high production rates, the EU would be able to do something similar in that it could control an even larger amount of the world's money supply due to its exceptional services and use it to create growth internally. States and regions within the EU that would otherwise lack the financial bargaining power on their own would be able to benefit from the collectively stronger position of the EU in order to negotiate better deals for themselves with outside markets and further reduce the regional disparity in wealth and even power. Furthering the reduction in discrepancies between EU regions would be more freedom within the EU; the internal movement policies already do that for most aspects of business but it is necessary to go further, especially concerning commerce and business. Banking services for instance need to be able to bridge the gaps between currencies more smoothly,

---

[17] European Union Committee on the Regions; "Delivering on the Europe 2020: Strategy Handbook for Local and Regional Authorities" 2012

allowing for different currencies to be debited from individuals' accounts in chip and pin services, for example, which would bolster the amount of commerce done internally. The single market seems to work fine for businesses and corporations, but it still has yet to become a true single market due to the apparently domestic commercial habits of consumers within the EU. Other initiatives such as Macro-Regional Strategies (MRTs) allow for better cooperation between states and regions, and could potentially be useful to promote the advancement of certain goals pertaining to reducing the disparities between EU regions. One MRT that has already been successful is the Baltic Region Strategy, and have been described as, "... a useful non-cost tool to better coordinate the existing available resources and to increase the effectiveness of investments"[18]. Further cooperation would be desirable to reduce differences in the EU, on a social, cultural, financial and political level.

One of the largest economic problems in Europe, which has resulted from a lack of infrastructure, especially in member-states that once had nominally socialist or soviet societies, is the scale of corruption in every part of society; in 2013 the estimated cost of corruption to the EU was estimated at 120 billion euros, which was only slightly less than that year's annual budget for the EU[19] although it may potentially be much higher[20]. Clearly this is a huge issue for the economy of Europe, and furthermore it flags up many regional disparities. The areas in the EU that have the most corruption according to the EC's report correlate almost identically with the countries that have the lowest GDPs in the EU[21]. According to the report the areas that are most at risk of

---

[18] Isabel Moran Vidal; "Macro-regional strategies across Europe"; EPRSLIBRARY; January 28, 2015; Quote by Rossella Rusc, from the Italian Permanent Representation of the European Parliamentary Research Service

[19] Report From The Commission To The Council And The European Parliament; EU Anti-Corruption Report; Brussels, 3.2.2014 Com(2014) 38 Final

[20] Communication From The Commission To The European Parliament, The Council And The European Economic And Social Committee; Fighting Corruption In The EU; Brussels, 6.6.2011 Com(2011) 308 Final

[21] The Data Team; "Taking Europe's pulse"; The Economist; Feb 13th 2015

corruption are construction, healthcare, academic institutions and tax administration, the latter being arguably of most concern. A good example of what corruption does to a Eurozone economy is Greece; from 1995 to 2008 Greece had one of the lowest total tax revenues in Europe[22], until the Greek debt crisis of 2009 when the government desperately attempted to collect the taxes that millions of Greeks owed, and it has increased steadily ever since. The lack of tax revenue, the cover-up of true national debt, corruption of tax officials, government authorities, local officials, the police, and corporations were major factors leading to plummeting confidence, not just in Greece's economy but the EU as a whole, as investors could no longer rely on the Greek economy.

Corruption, fraud and organised crime affect virtually every area of the EU, and prevent efficiency in the economy, and whilst growth may potentially increase due to the activities of these groups or individuals perpetrating these crimes, especially in eastern Europe where businesses creating infrastructure such as construction are often corrupt in some form[23], they probably do not pay taxes and the wealth that they earn does not "trickle-down" to the rest of the economy and the multiplier effect is most likely stunted. Therefore it is vital throughout Europe to combat such corruption and ensure successful and above all, stable, growth that does not leave the wealth in a few hands, but rather benefits the entire economy. Anticorruption initiatives are being taken all over the EU, with varying success, but some have achieved a lot, for example, in Romania which has one of the worst corruption problems in the EU, The Romanian National Anti-Corruption Directorate (DNA) has indicted over 4700 defendants with a 90.25% successful conviction rate from 2007-2014, many in high level positions and within the areas that the EC report highlights as high-risk areas[24].

---

[22] World Bank; "World Development Indicators: Tax Revenue" Feb 2015
[23] Ernst & Young; "Managing bribery and corruption risks in the construction and infrastructure industry" 2012 Ernst and Young Publications
[24] Report From The Commission To The Council And The European Parliament;

More initiatives and more specialised agencies across the EU are needed to tackle this issue and there are no reports on corruption within the mechanisms and institutions of the EU itself. Whilst much of the corruption in the EU is a result of inadequate infrastructure and, not necessarily, as the report by the EC highlights, many serious issues; even during its creation there were constant issues with the transparency of member states' records and finances and great resistance to what was generally considered "snooping" by the EC and potentially acting ultra vires by interfering with the domestic affairs of states. Stronger guarantees of integrity and transparency of state spending is required and more must be done, not just by member states, but by the EU as a whole to combat all illicit dealings, to restore faith in the EU and its markets. Furthermore it would mean that the EU would have a higher GDP overall and would result in more funding for EU projects, ironically including schemes to combat corruption, especially as the current EU fraud and corruption agency Olaf, has limited resources[25]. Not only would a more transparent Europe mean less illegal activity, it would also reduce regional disparity, with more funds for projects and more harmonious growth that can be quantified and measured accurately, allowing for better faith in the collective market and more growth in states' whose economies are stagnant and corrupt.

More can be done in the EU's administration to help reduce disparities in its regions. Raising public awareness of the functions and legislation of the EU would go a long way to helping its cause and aims of a single market, as currently only larger companies are able to take advantage of the commercial benefits the free market brings. The popularity of the EU is at an all-time low and it is vital that citizens stay informed of the EU's workings and benefits so as not to give rise to radicalisation of politics and to prevent states from potentially leaving the EU and plunging themselves and the

---

EU Anti-Corruption Report; Brussels, 3.2.2014 Com(2014) 38 Final; p.14
[25] Chris Morris; "Corruption across EU 'breathtaking' - EU Commission"; BBC News Online; 3 February 2014

region into another recession crisis. Citizens of the EU should know their rights better and understand the logic behind decisions made in Brussels. The EU should also encourage member states to make their economies more attractive to investors, both internal and external, especially those flagging behind, in order to boost growth and capital. Furthermore, increased investment in infrastructure in those states that are less developed should be undertaken and encouraged further by the EU, diverting funds not just to build in that state, as this can lead to complacency by governments that are being helped, but rather multinational projects, such as wind farms in multiple states, hydroelectric projects and research and development, including providing research centres for multinational use and academic institutions that focus on replicating the already sterling success of programs such as the Erasmus Project. This would allow for multi-state participation and growth, without treating the states in question as charity cases.

In conclusion, it has become clear that the EU must act decisively to strengthen its economic, social and political areas, or else risk preventing growth and enabling stagnation caused by corruption, and political outcry. It is necessary for the creases found within the EU to be ironed out and the divergence of economies and societies brought to a halt in order for the EU to not only prosper, but on a much darker note, survive its ills.

# ASHMITA KRISHNA
## - Regional Disparities and the Individual Member States... We Need a Liberal Approach

*"If I had an hour to solve a problem I'd spend 55 minutes thinking about the problem and 5 minutes thinking about solutions"* (Albert Einstein)

With the enlargement of the European Union; new countries, cultures and people were added to the European family. This has increased the heterogeneity between member states and regions. This effect was even multiplied by the recent economic crises. Some regions were more affected than others. Based on the different levels of economic and social development in Europe, a division can be made between three different groups. First of all, the prosperous and wealthy so-called Western group (e.g. Finland, Germany, UK and The Netherlands). A second group would be the periphery or less developed countries (e.g. Ireland, Spain, Greece, Italy) and lastly the former Eastern economies. The regional policy of the European Union consists of the promotion of integration and cohesion by reducing these regional disparities. The philosophy of the European policy makers is that a common market needs homogenous economic development. Therefore, even though the views on the success rate of those programs are mixed, one third of the total spend of the European Union is spent on decreasing regional differences.

In this paper I would like to argue that our valued European policy makers might not be tackling the real cause of the problem. By using a Six Sigma technique (a tool for process improvement) I would like to show that the real problem is not the increased economic disparities between our member states but a lack of understanding of the real problem which leads to a focus on the symptoms of this problem and therefore cannot be a solution. The real problem is a lack of focus and a focus on the wrong level. I also elaborate on the success rate of the regional policy of the European Union and use Ireland as an example here. Last but not least I would like to propose some solutions which could be worthwhile exploring.

## Making the European Union more lean

In process improvement one of the most popular tools is the 'five times why technique'. The five times why technique challenges the problem statement by asking a simple 'why?' five times. The idea behind it is that after the fifth 'why?' the real cause or core of the problem has been identified which should be the focus of the problem analysis. In this specific case the increased economic disparity between member states is seen as a problem. Why? Because inequality can lead to unrest, disunity and eventually disintegration. Why is this a problem? This is a problem because it threatens the current state of the European Union. Why should a threat to the current state of the European Union be a threat? Why can it not be an opportunity? The current European Union has achieved significant peace in the continental area and decreased the likelihood of conflicts. The European Union was initially erected to have additional economic as well as social benefits. Why would we need that? Because these freedoms have enriched and empowered the lives of the individual citizens of the European Union.

## The individual member states and Europe

Policies should therefore enrich and empower the individual. If we look at the current policies of the European Union to decrease regional disparities, can we identify these individual empowering elements? The Treaty of Lisbon has failed as an attempt to focus on decentralization as argued by Nicola (2011)[26] because of a focus on EU-wide procedures instead of understanding how different legal and geographical factors characterize each territory within each

---

[26] Nicola, F. (2011). The False Promise of Decentralization in EU Cohesion Policy. Tulane Journal of International & Comparative Law, 20, 65.

member state. In other words, there is a lack of understanding of the unique characteristics of each member state. Nicola suggests that a more contextualized and needs-based approach to cohesion policies, which acknowledges territorial and socio-economic disparities in each region, would anticipate and evade the shortcomings of current EU cohesion policy. And how successful has the overall regional policy of the European Union been? Becker (2012)[27] shows in his article that not all regions are equally good at converting convergence transfers into additional growth in case the education level of the workforce is below average, or government is of poor quality, which will lead to ineffective and poor use of limited funds. Lastly he argues that when the transfer intensity exceeds the maximum desirable level, no additional growth is generated by additional transfers. His recommendation is therefore to have the transfer under the EU's Regional Policy to be limited to the maximum desirable level of around 1.3% of a recipient region's GDP.

**The case of Ireland**

I would like to use the article of Quinn (2014)[28] for an illustration of how well the regional policy of the European Union has worked so far. For Ireland, EU regional policy has served since the 1970s. The infrastructure has been improved, as well as human resources and entrepreneurship. And even though the average Irish man's quality of life might have been improved, Quinn shows with a data analyses over the regions in the period 1981 – 2011 that regional disparities are still a fact. Also take into account that by the end of 2008, Ireland had received over €17 billion in Structural Funds. The case of Ireland reminds me of charity where we all transfer millions of dollars every year to organizations and those in need and might improve the life of a few without solving the actual problem.

---

[27] Becker, S. O. (2012). EU Structural Funds: Do they generate more growth. The CAGE-Chatham House Series, (3).
[28] Quinn, B. (2014). Resources and resourcefulness: Ireland and EU regional policy.

## The member state as the customer

Concluding, I would like to end with a recommendation based on the three step model that Farole, Rodríguez-Pose, & Storper, (2011) [29] use in their article. A true cohesion policy does not focus itself on reducing the gap in GDP per capita across regions but combating under development which promotes both local and EU growth. This asks for diversification: there is no one-size-fits all solution, the context (e.g. regional, local) is important. Thirdly they stress the importance of having strong institutions which can enforce these developments. Without proper checks and balances weak regions will keep surviving. The current situation with Greece is an excellent example of that.

---

[29] Farole, T., Rodríguez-Pose, A., & Storper, M. (2011). Cohesion policy in the European Union: Growth, geography, institutions. JCMS: Journal of Common Market Studies, 49(5), 1089-1111.

# DANIEL HINŠT
# - Getting Back to Growth: Clues for Europe in a Global Economy

## The liberal legacy

Liberals have always had clear policy positions for restoring growth in Europe. Our liberal friends in member states and on the EU level have used their influence to promote the growth agenda for Europe. I will emphasize the legacy of liberal policy in Estonia.

## More single market

There is a broad consensus in the EU that we can reach high growth potential with further market integration and liberalisation. On the internal market, continuing to remove regulatory obstacles to businesses, especially by more ambitious implementation of the Services Directive (implementation still not over). On the external side: creating conditions for free trade with USA. TTIP is our chance for additional growth gains.

Liberals are quite reserved about predicting exact economic growth gains. However, we know that every market opening, especially when exemptions from free trade principles are minimized, contributes to growth. This means TTIP is a good idea. If it is so easy, why does it need to be so hard? The answer lies in populism and opposition to liberal solutions. Everybody wants growth and jobs, but not everyone wants sound market policies to promote growth and more business opportunities, based on innovation, private investment and free trade. This is our liberal advantage in politics.

We need to be reserved about inflation of requests for exemptions from TTIP. This is the same story as with our single market for services. If not a 100% free market, it should not legitimize the goal to create only 70% market freedom. We can still think about at least 95%, and even more.

TTIP is a great long-term opportunity to set conditions for a transatlantic single market. Exempting audiovisual and public services from transatlantic liberalisation is a step to conserve socialism. Liberals need to promote the free will of consumers, instead of selfish bureaucratic judgements on what needs to be "protected". Sure, we need to protect European freedom from bureaucratic interventions and instead promote market oriented public policy management.

## Better regulation as the priority

One of the top EU priorities is better regulation. Certainly this does not mean more regulation, but regulatory quality in policy making. Member states such as the Netherlands and the UK are the frontrunners in this initiative. Regulation can be useful if it is very small and horizontal in its scope and focused on creating broad and open conditions for free market. Regulation needs to be simple, proportionate and justified. The EU has a strong proportionality principle in its regulatory policy which needs to be implemented in practice. A comprehensive (less and) better regulation and deregulation agenda is a huge opportunity because reducing and eliminating the administrative burden can bring additional growth. Regulation costs a lot and steals the property rights of those who create new value. Therefore, assessing impact of regulation, measuring regulatory costs and cutting the red-tape is for sure the cure for growth. It is the task of the EU-level lawmakers and those in member states. Regulatory cooperation is also an important part of the TTIP agenda for cutting the red-tape and promoting harmonisation on both sides.

## Digital single market

The next potential area is the digital aspect of our European single market. DSM is an excellent opportunity also because our liberal friend Andrus Ansip is now the Commission's vice president for this area. Estonian solutions in e-governance can be our guide for a better Europe.

Jobs are going digital and e-business is (or should soon become) a regular thing for maintaining competitiveness. Governments may be slower than businesseses in adapting e-govt and open data solutions. However, in order to promote growth, policies should aim at creating the 2nd generation Points of Single Contact (EUGO network) and removing anti-digital administrative barriers. The aim is to improve of the mechanisms for starting business and especially startups. Education reforms should primarily be focused on more private education, more digital skills and the e-learning agenda.

## Conclusions

Liberal solutions for growth are relatively simple. However, we do not offer blind faith that policy making can solve all of the problems. It is also up to every individual to take responsibility for growth. The role of our governments in Europe should be to downsize its bad influences whenever and wherever they block our liberal dreams.

We want very easy conditions to start new businesses. It is often the case that some bureaucrats do not share the same thoughts. They rather want control over the process. In the meantime, those same bureaucrats will blame many other things, including liberalism, for the lack of growth.

This is our challenge to promote responsible policies which will enable easy market access for everyone, not just for the chosen ones. Our Europe has a good future which mostly depends on us and our courage to combat barriers to growth. We believe that growth is up to creative potentials of numerous individuals who take their risks in order to satisfy our needs and improve the quality of our living.

# EGIJA GAILUMA
# - Getting Back to Growth: Clues for Europe in a Global Economy

It is not a secret that Europe is under pressure right now. Diminishing growth year by year, political sanctions, austerity, Euro crisis, large debts, regional disparities and more. It is frightening when we think of all these problems since eventually they have an impact on our lives as individuals. If we try to look deeper than just assuming that Europe has lost its solvency then we might find out the reasons and the path of this problem sequence. It all started somewhere in history. We can see in the table below that the growth problems did not start during the financial recession.

## The slowdown
Real GDP growth rate by decade, %

| Country | 1960s | 1970s | 1980s | 1990s | 2000s |
|---|---|---|---|---|---|
| Spain | 110.0 | 42.0 | 31.1 | 31.1 | 24.1 |
| Britain | 33.9 | 28.0 | 33.3 | 29.7 | 19.7 |
| US | 49.5 | 38.8 | 35.9 | 37.4 | 17.3 |
| Netherlands | 60.3 | 39.8 | 21.2 | 36.9 | 14.9 |
| France | 70.4 | 41.9 | 25.8 | 20.7 | 11.7 |
| Germany | 53.5 | 39.4 | 22.9 | 22.3 | 8.4 |
| Italy | 76.9 | 43.6 | 27.6 | 16.1 | 4.1 |

Source: OECD

Growth rates for the major European countries were significant but then it started to diminish; competition might be one of the reasons for this. At the same time, on November 1, 1993, the European Union was founded with an aim of accelerating growth and stimulating cooperation. Then we can take a look at a table of the same data but adding some more countries and years.

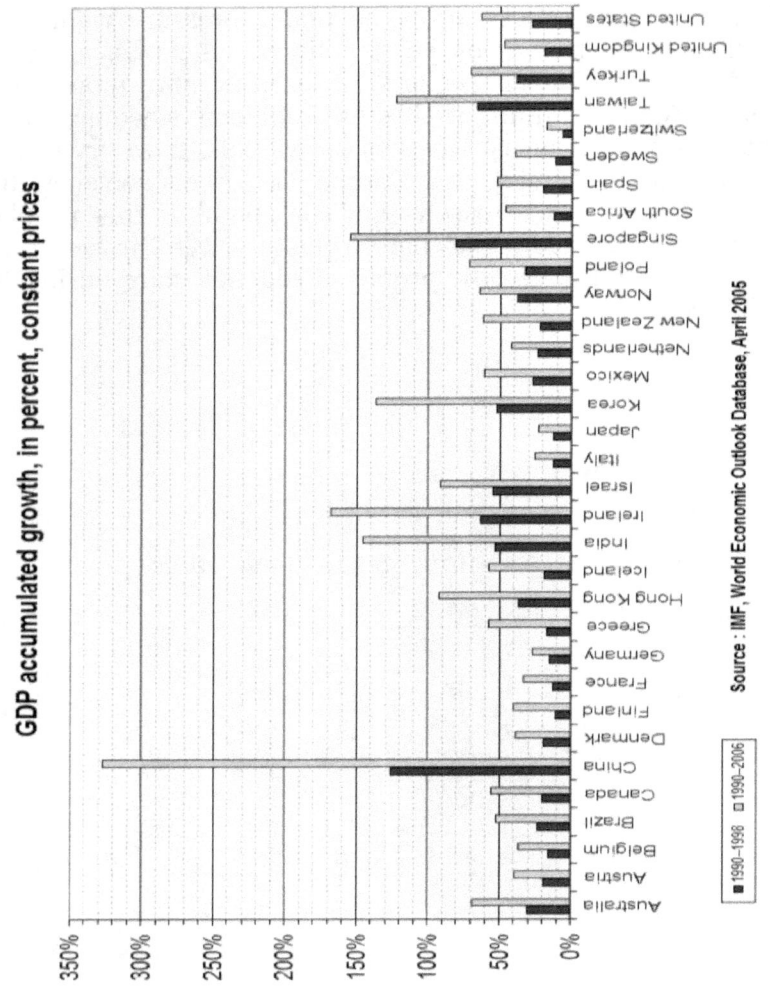

Here we can clearly see that one country is a top runner – China. It made its way through the tough markets and was able to provide the whole world with cheap labour. However, we can see that Europeean countries have increased their growth after the establishment of the EU. In the fourth quarter of 2014, the euro zone as a whole grew by 0.3%, and its biggest economy, Germany, expanded by 0.7%. The European Commission is forecasting growth in 2015 of 1.3%, which would be the euro area's best outcome since 2010.

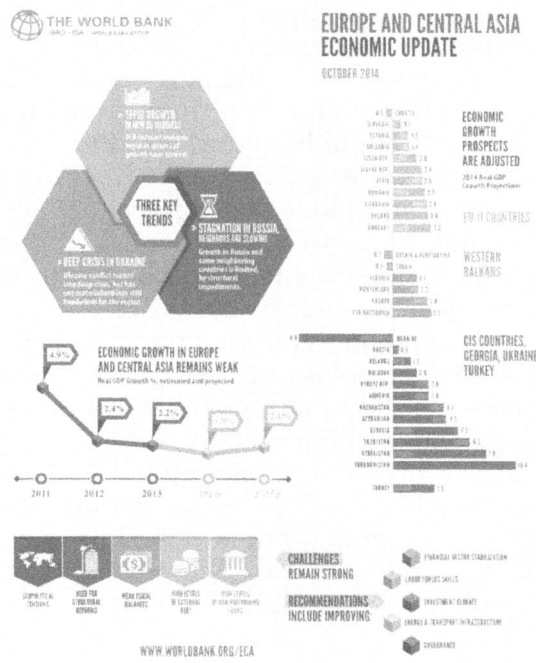

Although we have to be careful since France and Italy have been stagnating in the final quarter of 2014. Greece is actually a real threat for the stability of Europe. The consequences of all the problems may be very severe as the currency deflation and the machine has been turned on: prices are falling in Germany, Italy and Spain. The ECB is trying to escape the already running machine by implementing different kind of programs in order to boost prices back towards previous levels.

So, where did the meltdown start and why did it happen? One of the answers is the debt crisis, which is also what makes it so difficult to manage. The only way to get over it is to accelerate the growth but what can we do if Europe cannot make it happen, precisely because of the debt and all the other subsequent problems. It is like a magic circle that goes around and around. What we can do is to look at what aspects are holding Europe away from getting out of this loop. One of the reasons is demography. According to statistics, the European demography is not so impressive. Fertility rates are declining and countries like Germany are opening their borders for immigrants from Eastern European countries in order to keep their exports and services up to the scale where they can earn quantitatively. It means that the workforce is stagnating and ageing but Europe took on more debt anyway, which makes no sense. Due to this slowdown in the population governments are experiencing tougher times as the tax base is smaller and as such, there is less tax revenue. In addition, the current tax-financed systems of social pensions and health care will require substantial increases in the already high tax rates. The stagnation in workforce drives stagnation in the whole economy since the working capital is the seed of the growth. Stagnation would and is decreasing the attractiveness of Europe as an investment place. Combining all of these factors, one can truly argue that Europe is becoming really unsustainable and ask if anyone would want to invest in something so unsustainable and too risky with no risk-free guarantees.

One of the challenges that Europe has to overcome in order to become sustainable again is to address intra-euro area variance of competitiveness. Secondly, the European Investment Bank should invest more and more in sustainable projects and to accelerate the growth of those countries that are struggling with development. Thirdly, there are still some glitches with the banking system of

Europe; it has to become more solvent by properly implementing more long-term policies and investment funds.

Taking into account that the political crisis that has overtaken the whole world has made Europe weaker, and the emerging European markets are slowly dying due to the conflict, the west is trying to help, but it is struggling with its own slowdown, thus it makes the whole of Europe more unstable.

The World Bank has made a very intimidating info-graphic which depicts the scary truth. It can be seen on the following page. It depicts everything that is going on right now; comments are redundant here.

As one can see, then, this depiction reveals the scary truth of the emerging Europe. We have discussed the problems that the whole of Europe is facing and then, additionally to these, are the setbacks driven by one player but that result in all players suffering. The whole world is like a sports team, if one team member is not playing, and is creating gaps in the defence, then the whole team tries to close the gap while opening up another one elsewhere. It happens like that in the world market and economy as well, which makes me, as the author, believe that Europe has no hope for a global economic growth while this hole in the economy with emerging markets stays open and while the political tensions haven't been unsettled.

Also Hans Timmer (Chief Economist in the World Bank's Emerging Europe and Central Asia region) said: "The forecast for the Emerging Europe and Central Asia region remains tepid because of deferred structural reforms, as well as ongoing weak growth in Western Europe and stagnation in Russia". Additionally, he has expressed that no country can be sustainable in the long run without economic growth, shared prosperity that is fiscally affordable, environmentally and socially responsible.

Now, let's discuss the future: the scary and unpredictable future of Europe. So, the euro has dropped to its lowest value in nine years while the US dollar is appreciating. According to the data, Europe holds 25% of the world's economy or global trade as we like to express it. 25% is a quarter of the 100%, but by size, Europe is not a quarter of the world, which indicates that Europe is essential to the world's market. Taking all of this into account, we must realize that if Europe's economy collapses there may be harsh outcomes. Experts and researchers are not betting that Europe will have a great near future because of its unemployment rates, high taxes, and that the strongest economies, such as Germany, are weakening. The ECB is implementing different strategies but at the same time creating a strict austerity for member states, which creates a controversial situation. Some countries have to tighten their belts while at the same time they have to spend more in order to boost the economy in their country, so that the money would circulate and generate new money. Europe is not investing enough in its infrastructure, which is one of the driving forces of development and investment attraction. Europe is facing enormous problems and difficulties, which makes for little optimism in 2015.

The other thing that we might consider is the governing body. Those people that have been elected to the European Parliament, are those the ones that are the smartest and wisest people? Have they been elected in a fair way? Is there a difference between the turnout of the national elections of EU member countries and the turnout of European Parliamentary elections? The results on average indicate that the turnouts differ in almost every case by a double-digit number of percentage points. In addition to answering this question the author also studied the reasons for this outcome, which will be described in more detail in the following paragraphs.

One of the reasons for the divergence is the lack of understanding of European governmental bodies, which leads to the inability to decide on which way to cast votes; hence, fewer people show up. This is followed by Ferejohn and Fiorina (1974) who argue even further that the regret index for not going to the EU elections is lower than for national parliamentary elections since people's home country is a higher priority.

Next, the electorate is rather sceptical about the promises that the future MEPs make since representation in the EP is small for every country; hence, the politicians cannot use the strategy of promising benefits to those regions (in this case own country) that vote for them, because of the trouble of enforcing their own will by having a minority in the EP. This statement is further supported by the empirical findings that did not show a clear correlation of the number of seats and turnout for EU elections.

Finally, since expressive values are much higher for national parliaments, because of their higher association with the electorate as "their home", EU elections lose voters who go there because of a feeling of patriotism. In addition, findings show that the longer a country has been in the union, the higher the turnout, which could imply that in the long run this value tends to grow.

Adding all of this together, we might consider that we have found sufficient evidence of the existence of a difference between national and EU elections, with numerable explanations of why this has happened.

Wrapping it all up, we can make something like an info-graph to show how countries in the EU end up with problems as large of those of Greece, Italy, Portugal, Spain or any other. Entering the euro zone → risk of devaluation decreases to zero → eventually lower interest rates → credit boom due to the cheap money → consumption and investment boom → employment grows, overheated labour market → wages up, costs up, prices up→ loss of competitiveness→ loss of exports, loss of jobs, high unemployment → loss of tax revenue, big budget deficits, rising debt→ debt crisis, high interest rates due to risk of default, austerity needed, no possibility to devalue → serious economy and growth problems that we are encountering right now. One might think that because of such possibilities the EU is implementing different kinds of treaties such as the treaty on stability, coordination and governance in the economic and monetary union, "Fiscal Compact", that should control countries in a way that aims to avoid these kinds of problems. Unfortunately, this is not the case. In a way, it helps with the inflation rate and some rules, but it does not impact the growth slowdown; which continues and which austerity cannot stop or cause it to increase again.

So, what should Europe do in order to regain its power and outgrow the rest of the world? There may be several options:

- Common legislation regarding new enterprises in each member country. For instance, micro-companies (very small enterprises) should have low taxes, such as those that are in present in some countries already. It should be the case all over Europe in order to stimulate people to do their small business officially, helping to decrease the shadow economy;
- Clearance on the tax system within the member countries and developing countries. It would stimulate trade with developing countries for resources and raw materials that can be used for manufacturing in the member countries. Developing countries are often struggling with providing these materials due to the tough tax system with the EU;
- Infrastructure is the key for all growth. Infrastructure in finance, logistics and information flow. It has to be made easy, open and secure in order to make member countries safe and insured about their trades and manufacturing;
- Endowment funds are necessary to be made for organizations and movements in order to ensure money in case of emergency or development. The EU should make it a mandatory requirement for organizations that have more than a certain amount of people they are protecting or representing;
- Laws regarding entrepreneurship, exiting business and returning to it, have to be made simpler and easier to cooperate with.

There are many small things that could be done in order to improve the quality of the EU and Europe as a whole. The situation is as it is in its economy's life cycle. Nothing lasts forever, even stability and growth. There are some peaks and downturns; it's just the way the life cycle is. We have to accept it and be smarter when we are creating future plans. We need to take into account that something unexpected might happen. The key point for the government is to spend money when there is an economy downturn and save it when there is an economic peak. By spending in bad times we are ensuring that money is still within the economy and businesses do not have to exit; they can tighten their belts, but it does not mean they must shut down. While saving in good times means that the money is enough for businesses to cope by themselves and we can make some reserves to spend in bad times since the day will come. Each country in Europe has to understand this and continue investing in its development and use all the possibilities that the EU is providing.

Greece and Italy cannot fail without devastating much of Europe. Europe cannot suffer without causing problems in China. China cannot slow down without causing major problems in the rest of the world. Everything is connected.

Europe will outperform the US in upcoming years if it continues to pursue its goals and does not start printing money, just to stay in business today without thinking about tomorrow. The EU in 2020 has to be made a priority and everyone has to stick to it otherwise the growth will come slower than it should.

# FELIX GIEßMANN
## - Challenges and Opportunities of the EU Energy and Resource Efficiency Policy

The EU has long recognised that natural resources are a major production factor and an important base for our wealth. That a sustainable and efficient way to use our remaining natural resources is a key factor of a sustainable future for the European Union. The Treaty on the functioning of the European Union promotes, "energy efficiency and energy saving and the development of new and renewable forms of energy" and the, "interconnection of energy networks." However, Article 194 of the TFEU does not grant the European Union with the legislative competence to implement energy policy measures that would affect the "Member States' right to terming the conditions of exploiting its energy resources; Member States' choice between different energy sources; and the general structure of a Member States' energy supply"; despite Climate change, security of supply and affordability are an European, not a national matter.

The European Union implemented several legal acts towards a common European Energy Market: The first liberalisation package unbundled the market, the second one liberated market access and the third and most recent package introduced national regulatory authorities and a corresponding forum on an European level ("Agency for the Cooperation of Energy Regulators"). The EU set ambitious goals for the energy transition: by 2020 the resource efficiency shall be 20% higher and $CO_2$-Emmissions 20% lower.

The Commission expects the power grid to expand more than 52.000km by 2025, but the implementation faces huge challenges on a regional level. In some parts of the EU the energy transition seems to be stuck, for example Germany: Citizen's movements and political action committees prevent a progressive approach of a High-voltage direct current network, which enables the green power of the north of Germany to replace the missing energy due to the nuclear phase-out since 2011.

Poland's government demands to stay with old coal power plants as a reliable energy source due to its huge natural reserves of coal, and the Mediterranean member countries' solar energy initiative does not meet expectations. We face many problems of the implementation of the EU energy and resource efficiency policy due to the restriction of the topics of the European Union. There is a wide-range of different national regulation in the electricity sector: Some countries have renewable energy targets (e.g. Germany, UK, France & Spain), feed-in tariffs and premium payments, tradable renewable energy certificates, fiscal incentives and public financing.

A harmonisation of the support schemes is absolutely necessary, but the future outlook is disappointing. a full EU energy market liberalisation leading to harmonised electricity costs is unlikely, e.g. France is highly regulated and the UK very liberalised. A sufficient European grid capacity between member states of the European Economic Area and Switzerland is slowly improving, but still very limited.

We need a coordinated European energy policy to have a better outlook concerning energy dependency, affordable prices and a high reliability. The European Union and its citizen could save billion of Euro if the European Union as a major player could handle energy contracts and treaties.

And we have to consider not only the cost of production but the overall cost of energy to society. The choice of energy solutions needs proper multiple-criteria decision aid, as an extremely high number of factors have to be considered: the social impact, the transmission reliability, compensation payments for citizens, subsidies, the environmental impact, the employment and health impact. This can't be done by the member states alone and needs a proper harmonisation on standards and measurements for the whole European Economic Area.

We have to achieve renewable energy production happening in the perfect geographic location in the EU. It is very questionable that there are high subsidies for photovoltaic power in Germany, as the money could be used for a much higher output if installed in the Mediterranean (Portugal, Italy, Greece and Spain) or we could save billions of Euros for the same energy output. Wind-energy will reach its maximum efficiency as offshore power plants in the North and the Baltic Sea, not in the central inland of the continental EU. Savings of up to €80 billion are expected, while approximately €20 billion need to be invested for a power transmission grid. The EU should consider this option as an investment of the European Regional Development fund.

There are major economical advantages, providing opportunities for the Baltic and Mediterranean member states (I don't want to use the infamous term PIGS: Portugal, Italy, Greece and Spain).

The European Union should reshape the World's energy production by being the flagship of renewable energy resources and remaining competitive and the same time. This is a very difficult goal to achieve, but over the long term, we will benefit from independent, renewable and clean energy sources. The economic potential is huge, as we could save up to 60 billion Euros within the next 15 years. On the other hand, we should not forget that our industry highly depends on reliable and affordable power and to consider that power price is a deciding factor for companies with energy-intensive processes. The European Union can't compete internationally with its high energy prices, the average kWh for companies is almost twice as big as the United States. But we can strengthen the economy with resource efficiency policies and technology to help the companies reduce its energy consumption.

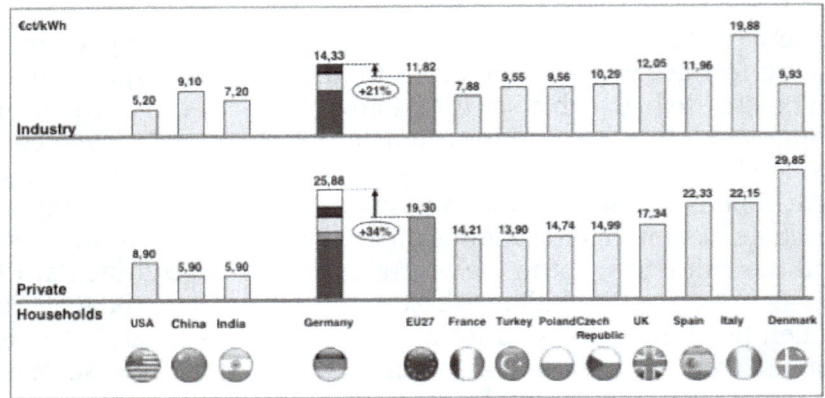

Furthermore there is already a huge variety of EU and regional policies which is difficult to see as an overview. In Germany's state North-Rhine Westphalia alone I can mention a few different initiatives and regional actors in the intermediary system, some of them heavily funded by the EU; which have the same goal, resource efficiency and climate change:

Klima Expo NRW, Orte des Fortschritts (Locations of Progress), Energieagentur.NRW (Energy Agency), Effizienzagentur.NRW (Efficiency Agency) etc. that could be consolidated, to provide companies easier access to information and implementation aid.

I conclude that the EU needs further harmonisation of the energy and resource efficiency policy, an easier to overview regulatory context and more competencies for the European Commission to achieve the 20/20/20-Goals.

**Sources:**
- Challenges of EU Energy Policy, Siemens AG, 2014
- Connecting Possibilities: Scenarios for Optimizing Energy Systems, Siemens AG, 2013
- Treaty on the functioning of European Union, CELEX:12012E/TXT

# FELIX REIMANN
## - European Financial Accounting as a Factor for Transparency and Economic Growth

In 2002, the EU Parliament (EP) passed a regulation that requires consolidated and simple accounts for all companies listed in the EU to use International Financial Reporting Standards (IFRS) for fiscal years starting after January 1, 2005. This widespread adoption of IFRS caused a fundamental change in the European business environment, especially in the availability of information. Prior to 2005 companies had to follow a variety of country-specific Generally Accepted Accounting Standards (GAAP) making it difficult for investors to compare firms in different countries. The objective of this EU Directive was to harmonize the Financial Reporting within the EU, and thus improve the investment quality and transparency within the EU. However, in the context of the European IFRS implementation, it is first helpful to consider the objectives of the International Accounting Standards Board (IASB) and the European Commission (EC) regulators. Furthermore it is important to understand the mechanisms on which regulatory change in Europe relies.[30]

The IFRS are a set of accounting standards published by the IASB. The primary objective of the IASB is to develop, in the public interest, a single set of high quality, understandable and enforceable global accounting standards that require high quality, transparent and comparable information in financial statements and other financial reporting to help participants in the world's capital markets and other users to make economic decisions. Furthermore the IASB promotes the use and rigorous application

---

[30] Soderstrom, N. S., & Sun, K. J. (2007). IFRS adoption and accounting quality: a review. *European Accounting Review*, 16(4), 675-702. Available at http://goo.gl/UhJVPs

of those standards. Following these objectives the IASB has to be seen as a strong international lobby. [31]

The European Union is perhaps the most important organization to emerge as a source of demand for international harmonization based on International Accounting Standards (IAS). Before the adoption of IFRS in the EU the EC tried to harmonize GAAP by providing a set of broad guidelines using Directives. These Directives focused on the content and form of accounts, audit requirements, and accounting measurement principles, and allowed various options reflecting the diversity of practices across Europe at the time in order to achieve agreement across Member states. As a result, these guidelines were ineffective in promoting any significant convergence of financial reporting practices across Europe. For that reason the EC considered establishing an EU accounting-standard setter. This would have been a substantial obstacle to international regulation convergence. For that reason the European Commission decided to adopt the IFRS to further a single financial market across the EU to contribute growth and employment opportunities. Comparability of financial statements through common reporting standards was considered to be a priority in achieving the aim of the single financial market. Additionally, the reporting standards should be transparent, fully understood, properly audited and effectively enforced. The Commission also defines qualities of financial reporting information that it regards as important, including relevance, timeliness, reliability and comparability. There is a close association between the principles of the EC and the IASB agenda. Given this congruence the EC recommended the adoption of the International Accounting Standards. This solution had the advantage of achieving harmonization within Europe as part of a broader initiative towards international harmonization. The justification surrounding the proposals for harmonization based on the IFRS referred to economic growth and employment opportunities, and therefore it seems that there was a belief that accounting harmonization would have favorable consequences for

---

[31] IFRS Foundation (2013): Constitution, Available at http://goo.gl/O6QXIQ

product and labor markets. There was hope that the adoption of IFRS would reduce the cost of capital and that it would lead to more efficient capital allocation and greater cross border investment, thereby promoting growth and employment in Europe.[32]

Transparency in the financial markets is a crucial issue for a society as a whole. Over the last decades an increasingly large number of individuals have poured money into domestic and foreign stock markets through pension and mutual funds. Thus, transparent company accounts are beneficial to individual investors as well as institutional investors. The global financial crisis has shown once again that a lack of transparency in the financial markets results in a widespread fall in investors' confidence which will lead to liquidity shortages and stock market crashes. For this reason the enforcement of IFRS within the EU is of critical importance. The IFRS are only helpful for an investors' decision making if every firm's financial statement within the EU has to meet the same quality criteria. This is the same with any law: the rules are only effective if they are enforced properly and evenly. Uneven enforcement of IFRS in European countries can be a problem for firms with incentives to produce high quality financial statements (e.g. firms with high growth opportunities and financing needs) but residing in countries with weak enforcement. These firms have difficulties signalling their high quality financial reporting to the market. The Enforcement process within the EU is different for each member state and there is a great diversity of practices across Europe about how much information of the enforcement process is made public. This leads to overall loss of confidence in many parts of the European enforcement system. This problem has to be tackled to improve the capital market within the EU with the benefit of higher growth and employment rates. Additionally, transparency in financial statements is only achieved if two criteria are met. First, the set of rules under which

---

[32] Devalle, A., Magarini, R., & Onali, E. (2014). Assessing the Value Relevance of Accounting Data after IFRS Introduction in Europe. Available at http://goo.gl/l7RgxT.

a financial statement is made has to be publicly known. Every investor can only interpret the result of complex equations in the form of a financial statement. This interpretation gets more precise the more is known about the equations.

Second, the enforcement of rules under which these equations emerge has to be relatively constant. This is especially true the more complex these rules become. By now the revenues of the same firm under the IFRS can be different if the firm resides e.g. in Ireland or Germany. [33]

A reform of the European enforcement system is necessary to provide comparability between firms within the EU and transparency to the public. Such a reform has to take certain aspects into account (e.g. creating competition between different enforcement agencies to offer higher quality enforcement). At the risk of over-simplifying what could be a quite complex piece of EU legislation, this Directive, should require member states to pass legislation to enable firms to the same enforcement that they would have in another member state. If a member state X is not able to provide a certain enforcement quality to a given firm, this firm would be given a right to opt in the financial reporting oversight system of member state Y. The National Enforcer of country x would then be obliged to pay the expected costs associated with review and enforcement. By implementing this process within the EU, firms would be able to benefit from the best financial reporting oversight available. This proposal would have several potential advantages, particularly in creating competition between different enforcement agencies to offer higher quality enforcement where it was efficient to do so, but to cede regulatory authority to more efficient agencies if local inefficiencies and cost disadvantages, e.g. related to the supply of local expertise, could not be overcome.[34]

---

[33] Brüggemann, U. (2011). Intended and unintended consequences of mandatory IFRS adoption. In *Essays on the economic consequences of mandatory IFRS reporting around the world* (pp. 5-43). Gabler. Available at http://goo.gl/Kc8sje

[34] Pope, P. F., & McLeay, S. J. (2011). The European IFRS experiment:

Harmonizing the different GAAP within the EU by implementing a single set of standards provided a sustainable improvement to information quality and thus investment quality. The effectiveness of the adoption of the IFRS and its positive effects on European economic growth is limited by local diversities in financial reporting enforcement quality. After the convergence of European GAAP after the EU wide implementation of IFRS, the harmonization of the European financial regulation enforcement systems is the logical next step to further improve the European capital market and to grow together as a European family.

---

Objectives, research challenges and some early evidence. *Accounting and business research*, *41*(3), 233-266. Available at http://goo.gl/K3u3oF

# IGOR CALDEIRA
## - Why Portuguese Municipalities Fail: breaking vicious circles to promote growth

### §1 – *Theoretical approach*

In this article I intend to analyse, and propose a feasible alternative, to the current state of local governance in Portugal. I use a neo-institutionalist approach, that is – I assume that citizens and institutions are not pure rational actors, not inherently good or bad, but simply that they react to the environment they are in. Normative and historical institutionalism implies that actors not only mould, but are also moulded by institutions (state, companies, laws, culture, religion, technology, etc.) and that the same actors, under different incentives will have different reactions. Also, paths chosen in the past format paths chosen in the present, though a mix of hazard and volition can change the future (meaning, despite the influence of context, that there is no deterministic dogma).

The title of this article is borrowed from the book *Why Nations Fail*, by Acemoglu and Robinson[35]. Following the general principles of neo-institutionalism, the central thesis of this book is that man-made institutions are more relevant for economic and political outcomes than past racial, geographic or dialectical determinisms have tried (and failed) to prove. A crucial distinction is made between *inclusive* versus *extractive* institutions. Inclusive institutions are those that promote the biggest participation possible of members of the political community, which also implies, necessarily, decentralization of powers and resources. Extractive institutions are those that concentrate the powers of decision (and the economic benefits) in the hands of the few.

---

[35] Daron Acemoglu and James A. Robinson, *Why Nations Fail – The Origins of Power, Prosperity and Poverty*, Crown Publishers, 2012.

Though there is no determinism, the authors do assert that both generate either virtuous spirals or vicious circles.

*I will here try to prove that Portugal's municipalities are stuck in a vicious circle that dooms their role and the country as a whole, but that small changes could help change the course of History.*

## §2 – *The context*

Portugal rejects, in its constitution, the possibility of federalization; under Article 6, it is a unitary state, despite recognizing the autonomy of the two Atlantic archipelagos of Madeira and the Azores. This constitutional imposition of a unitary nature is not only legal, but actually finds echo in popular emotions: the 8th of November of 1998 referendum on the institution of regions was largely rejected (less than 35% of voters were in favour).

It is nothing to be surprised with: Portugal is linguistically one of the most uniform countries in Europe. There are no real dialects, and only a small language in its Northeastern corner[36] survives. Religious pluralism was eliminated by the Inquisition and the genocide of Sephardic Jews. Feudalism never had much of a chance in a country that went from centralized expansion to expel the Moors (1249), to a centralized maritime expansion (from 1415 onwards). Without Jews and with an oppressive Catholic morality over economic affairs, there was no bourgeoisie. With an aristocracy dependent on royal favours to pursue their extractive economic activities in India, Africa and Brazil, there was no opposition to the crown. Enlightenment did not change this: when the aristocrats tried to kill the king to indirectly attack its minister, the Marquis of Pombal (one of the few politicians that tried to modernize the country in centuries, privileging a productive

---

[36] The Mirandese language, from the sub-group of Asturo-Leonese Iberian Latin languages. The Portuguese state recognized it as co-official language in 1998.

economy over the mere transport of goods from the colonies to trade them for manufactured goods produced in England and other Western countries[37]), they were executed in a public ceremony whose gory details need no description.

Liberalism (Constitutional Monarchy, 1820/1834-1910, First Republic, 1910-1926) tried to change this. From 828 municipalities (*concelhos*) in 1834, there was a reduction to 415 in 1842[38] (for comparison, nowadays there are 308)[39]. This was intended partly to allow a more uniform application of law (the modern state was now being built in Portugal) and partly because bigger local units would, in principle, be economically, politically and administratively, more self-sustainable.

The Republican movement had such feelings even more ingrained. The 1891 Manifesto of the Portuguese Republican Party aimed at achieving a Swiss federal model. The truth is nevertheless that, despite all ideological inclinations, the 1911 constitution again institutes a unitary state.

Federalism, and, indeed, any aspiration of decentralization disappeared with the right-wing dictatorship (1926-1974) and it was only with the 1976 constitution that the islands achieved some degree of autonomy, while the continental part of Portugal continued to have a centralized administration with relatively weak

---

[37] The 20th century Portuguese thinker António Sérgio wrotethat Portugal had always relied on a *transport economy* with no own production – something that Acemoglu and Robinson call the *extractive institutions* created by colonial powers. This model in Portugal started with Indian trade (16th century), continued with Brazil (17th-18th centuries) and Africa (19th-20th centuries). In some way, European structural funds have reproduced this chain of events, where external sources of wealth are channelled to the elite, with limited trickle-down effects to the rest of the population.

[38] Source, Revista Militar N.º 2515/2516 - August/September 2011, pp 1023 - 1078.

[39] This results in Portugal having municipalities five times larger than the European average. Still, the difference is that they are less powerful, as we shall see this later. For numbers on the size of municipalities, check http://www.ccre.org/docs/Nuancier2011Web.EN.pdf, p. 4.

municipalities and no real intermediate level of governance between the local and the national levels.

## §3 – *How municipalities have helped ruining the country*

Portugal has been living through an economic crisis for several years now. This crisis, though having found its tipping point with the financial crisis of 2007-2009, was waiting to happen for quite some years. It was the product of mass public and private debt, a debt that found no correspondence in the incipient economic growth of the years that followed the burst of the Dotcoms. Despite the Left-wing propaganda, accusing Brussels or the financial markets of the Portuguese crisis, and the Right-wing propaganda blaming it all on the centre-left Socialist Party, the hard truth is that this is the fourth international financial intervention in Portugal since 1976. All governing parties participated in the debt frenzy and instituted policies that would inevitably lead to bankruptcy, one year or another.

Local powers have an interesting role in this tragedy. Despite representing a small percentage of the overall public expenditure (14%, against an EU average of 27%)[40], they have heavily influenced the high levels of private debt.

As visible in the graphic[41] below, private debt in Portugal doubled between 1995 and 2004, reaching its peak of 225% of the GDP in 2012. This debt was not fundamentally due to investment. On the contrary, and like several other countries (though not with the same intensity as in Spain or the United States) Portugal suffered from a real estate bubble. The ratio of equity to debt is bad, both in the corporate and household sectors in the country, and, as some have argued[42], private debt can be much more burdening to economic growth than public debt.

---

[40] http://www.ccre.org/docs/Nuancier2011Web.EN.pdf, p. 6.
[41] Private debt in Portugal, 1995-2014. Source: Eurostat.

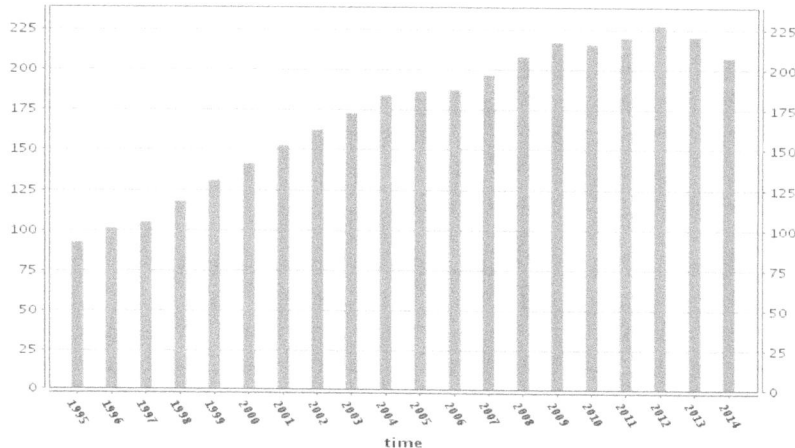

There is a close link between real estate speculation, private debt, corruption and the funding of municipalities in Portugal. Though the numbers of newly finished housing units has been dropping in the past ten years (no doubt the debt crunch and the financial crisis is playing its role here – the variation of private debt between 2005 and 2014 is relatively small), housing played a large role in the private debt boom. Not only did families indebt themselves, but so did companies. Overall, ten years ago investment in housing represented 8% of the GDP: three times the EU average[43]. At some point, the municipal zoning plans could allow new housing units for up to thirty million people – in a country that, if anything, is set to lose population in the coming decades (as it is already[44]).

Why is it so? Well, the theoretical approach adopted here implies that people are not irrational or stupid. They react to incentives. So what is the incentive for municipal authorities to be careless on

---

[42] http://www.economist.com/news/finance-and-economics/21588382-euro-zone-blighted-private-debt-even-more-government-debt-debtors.

[43] Numbers given by the president of a public company in Lisbon dedicated to urban rehabilitation, http://www.maisfutebol.iol.pt/imobiliario-portugal-habitacao-media-europeia/5474b4b93004dde856108fa7.html.

[44] The country lost 150000 people between 2011 and 2014: http://ec.europa.eu/eurostat/tgm/table.do?tab=table&init=1&language=en&pcode=tps00001&plugin=1.

issues such as private debt, for being permissive towards real estate promoters and building companies and for being so careless for good territorial planning (admitting that bulldozing green areas to build apartment blocks that will not be fully occupied in the foreseeable future is not good policy)?

Local governments are reacting to elements from the context they are in. And the context is, on the one hand, a massive dependency on money transfers from central authorities, especially in small-size municipalities[45]: on average, only 34% of their income comes from own resources. And then, crucially: of their own taxes, which constitute most of their incomes, municipalities depend on 75 to 82% on taxation of real estate[46].

| Taxes | Small municipalities | Medium municipalities | Larger municipalities | Total |
|---|---|---|---|---|
| Tax on real estate property | 62,8% | 65,6% | 56,4% | 60,5% |
| Tax on vehicles | 15,0% | 12,5% | 11,1% | 12,1% |
| Tax on real estate sales | 16,0% | 16,2% | 19,1% | 17,7% |
| Over-head tax on companies | 6,2% | 5,6% | 13,2% | 9,6% |
| Other taxes | 0,0% | 0,1% | 0,2% | 0,2% |
| Total | 100% | 100% | 100% | 100% |

Municipalities have to be keen on promoting the construction sector, even when it is economically irrational to do it, because the little financial independence they may have does not derive from

---

[45] http://pt.calameo.com/read/0003249818830e99d8443, p.35.
[46] Table adapted from ibid, p. 81.

productive, long-term investment in tradable goods that provide growth and jobs. Taxation over normal economic activities represents only 5 to 13% of their direct income[47]. Instead, and to ensure larger resources of their own, municipalities are lenient on real estate investors, who in turn also benefited from a too permissive credit policy from the banking sector in the years preceding the financial crisis.

Corruption, cross-interests between private and public affairs, and dubious party financing have also been a part of both national and local politics[48], with emphasis at a local level on the links between municipalities, building companies and often football clubs. The popular mood regarding corruption at a local level swings from the populist feeling "all politicians are the same" to verging on a cult of personality for the best-known corrupt mayors[49] . Local politicians, to ensure electoral wins, bet on non-productive (and often useless) public works such as roads or roundabouts - a technique not just from today but that has deep roots in the past[50].

---

[47] In Portuguese, 'derrama' – it is a percentage of the normal corporate tax that municipalities can charge above the tax already imposed by central government.
[48] See Transparency International, http://www.transparency.org/whatwedo/nisarticle/portugal_2012
pp. 5 and 6: "The neutrality of public institutions is also nigh on impossible during local elections. The fact that the current mayors may be candidates while still on political and executive duties has led to some abuses, namely the use of privileged information from the local administration offices (such as City Halls), or the usual openings and inaugurations during electoral campaigns, or even the illicit use of human and material resources of these local administration offices."
[49] Ibid, p.10: "Portuguese citizens [fall in the] logic of the 'efficient corrupt official' – one who 'steals from the public, but also gets the work done'. Such a short-sighted perspective on political performance promotes a lack of transparency and legal ambiguity, while simultaneously inhibiting public accountability of political actors for their crimes. This 'Robin Hood' style of corruption has a great level of acceptance within Portuguese society and is a symptom of a civic culture still founded on the satisfaction of the basic needs of daily life. In a 2006 survey of Portuguese citizens ca. 64 per cent of the respondents accepted corruption and bribery as long as it would benefit the public.3 Following this, it is not surprising that political candidates with pending corruption-related crimes are re-elected – sometimes with comfortable majorities [...]."
[50] As pointed out by José Cutileiro in its 1977 sociological and anthropological

These works provide inaugurations – visible ceremonies that are more appealing to voters than other more productive investments or on environmental protection.

### §4 – *You can't change people; but you can reform their context*

You don't need to be a pessimist about human ontology to realize that you are not going to change people's moral, social or political perceptions from one day to the other. You are also not going to transform an incompetent politician into an ace of management automatically. But you can certainly reduce the benefits from corruption and increase the potential gains from implementing good policies through some legal and institutional changes.

Throughout this article I have presented **numerous problems**: **a)** a centralized country with no traditions in decentralized power; **b)** an indebted country with a tradition of getting indebted; **c)** extractive institutions that are created by and reinforce a non-productive economy. This is then reflected at a local level in **d)** the absence of regional coordination of policies, **e)** municipalities whose resources and competences are limited, **f)** municipalities whose resources are too dependent mostly on national transfers and **g)** municipalities that are too dependent on incomes that come from sectors that produce non-tradable goods, and whose marginal reproductive effect is small as the country is mostly well served with the infra-structures needed for (road) transportation. Finally, **h)** the political culture and the array of competences in municipalities pushes actors to invest more in infra-structure and very little in sectors that can deliver economic benefits.

My **solutions for this are grounded on a change of incentives**. People in general, professional politicians in particular, love power and loath being dependent on someone else.

---

study of Southern Portugal (*Ricos e Pobres no Alentejo* - Rich and Poor in Alentejo). Public works were always a way of keeping the unemployed busy, even if it implied laying, dismantling, and relaying pavements.

So, naturally, local politicians will be inclined to stimulate those areas that will generate the most resources for their own municipalities. In the present scenario, those areas are related to the building sector. Whereas urban planning, zoning, are areas of natural competence of municipalities, it is also acceptable that incomes from those activities go to municipalities as well.

But there is no good reason why the present overhead *tax on corporate income* is not simply abolished, and substituted by a local tax on companies at the expense of the central government. For Liberals, this may seem blasphemous; wanting to impose more taxation on businesses. But what I am saying here is that the same tax level can simply be redistributed to the benefit of municipalities. Like it already happens, municipalities could determine the final amount of taxation, introducing a mechanism for fiscal competition. In return, municipalities would take more responsibility over areas where nowadays they are weak – such as education[51], a determinant factor for good economic performance.

Municipalities would then have a strong *incentive to promote productive economic activities*. Increased competences over education could also mean integration between the local economic tissue and schools (something that is generally feeble in Portugal) and the promotion of entrepreneurial skills in public schools (something that is practically non-existent presently).

A further rationalization of the construction sector could also be introduced by a change of the transfers from central government, introducing stronger environmental requests. Accepting that there is always some kind of trade off to be made between environment and development (though the two are far from opposed) it would be unfair to punish those municipalities that have a big portion of their territories limited to economic or urban development. Furthermore, and as we can see above in the table on own

---

[51] As seen in http://www.ccre.org/docs/Nuancier2011Web.EN.pdf, page 7, Portuguese Local municipalities spend 9,7% of their budget in education, half of the European average.

resources (demographically) bigger municipalities have twice as much income from corporate tax than smaller ones. Environmental considerations in income transfers would reduce the incentives for indiscriminate concessions on industries and give incentives for *a good balance between economic development and quality of life, while reducing regional asymmetries.*

## §5 – *Conclusions*

Having a centralized mode of governance is not, per se, a problem. Having weak municipalities is not, per se, a problem. In fact I argue that, because of the past and because of the popular feelings, talking about large-scale decentralization (or even, as I would personally prefer, in the line of the late Liberal period of Portugal, a Swiss federalization) in Portugal is pointless. It is not going to happen. But we do have a problem in the municipalities we have, in their practical action, regardless of their position in the overall governance of the country.

In this paper I tried to show that some of the challenges that the country has faced in the recent years have their roots in local governance, and that those roots have an institutional (legal, financial) nature. Since we cannot change human beings, and since we cannot do a complete institutional (i.e., constitutional) change of the country, my proposals are linked to some small changes in the sources of income of our municipalities.

Hopefully, the same way that local politicians have been so eager to participate in a construction frenzy that is completely unrelated to the capacity of the country and its citizens of borrowing money and that has no long-term effects in the country's economic sustainability, so they would, with my proposal, feel more inclined to look at which ways they could attract more businesses, or stimulate the creation of new ones.

Small changes can, in my opinion, break vicious circles and slowly start a virtuous cycle of growth. With a small change in their sources of income, *I believe that Portuguese municipalities could play a leading role in promoting growth, decentralizing economic power and reducing the regional asymmetries that have derived from centuries of political centralization.*

# JELENA JESAJANA
## - Regional Disparities: The case of Latgale

In modern discourse about inequality and disparity within the European Union, and Europe in general, we can often face the dichotomies of the north and the south, or the east and the west. In my opinion, however, it is possible to research the case of a small region in a small county, where one can find the same problems, tendencies, and often obstacles in fighting disparity. Namely, excessive dependence on the European Regional Development Fund, European Social Fund, Cohesion Fund; and lack of regional governments' incentives to stimulate small and medium enterprises, thus creating jobs and reasons for people not to emigrate.

Latvia, a small country in the Baltic region with the population of 2,067,887 people according to 2011 census[52], began its presidency of the Council of the European Union this January. Latvia is usually portrayed as a success story by Brussels bureaucrats: surviving the crisis with a rigid austerity measures and returning the economy to slight growth, all looking too promising and attractive. When Latvian Prime Minister – Laimdota Straujuma – was presenting the Presidency in front of the European Parliament, she was all of a sudden faced with harsh criticism, which manifested in UKIP Paul Nuttall MEP's accusations about rapid depopulation and huge emigration waves[53]. Though UKIP's views on problems in the EU are flawed (and must be discussed in a separate paper), here they are nonetheless right: Latvia is losing its population dramatically, partially due to high mortality and low birth rates, but even more so due to high emigration waves. During

---

[52] Demographics of Latvia by Latvian Central Statistics Bureau: http://data.csb.gov.lv/pxweb/lv/Sociala/Sociala__isterm__iedz/IE0010m.px/table/tableViewLayout1/?rxid=7ee5bb2b-7c93-4ccb-8a34-1aa4ade09cc3
[53] Paul Nuttall's speech http://www.ukip.org/an_old_tired_and_out_of_date_european_union

the last decade Latvia lost 14%[54] of its working-age population to emigration, who usually leave the country first, but then their families follow, so young children, potential professionals and future participants of the labor market, are lost too. The most popular destinations for Latvians are the UK, Ireland, and the rest of the EEA. Of course, the initial growth of emigration can be explained with the introduction of free movement after Latvia joined the EU in 2004; but an increase in emigration fell on the crisis and post-crisis periods, which can be explained with massive unemployment rates during that period – in 2009 the unemployment rate reached 25%[55] among males and 16% among females; particularly affecting the young, who are more mobile and hence more prone to emigration, and the non-Latvian ethnic minorities.

The combination of these two groups united in the region of Latgale, one of four Latvian historical and cultural regions, bordering Russia and Belarus, with the majority of the population speaking either Russian or Latgalian (a regional language). The second biggest city of Latvia is situated in Latgale – Daugavpils; the population of Latgale is 16% of the Latvian population, however there is no real official data measuring the real impact of emigration form the region, so the rest of the passage will be mostly based on private observations and journalist research. Historically Latgale was a region of farmers, with some big facility projects like the Hydroelectric station in Plavini, and several factories in wood production and car production. Beginning with the crisis of 2008 many Latvians emigrated to find jobs that they had lost at home, many of those seeking better living standards came from Latgale region. The effect of emigration is so strong, that there are several smaller towns in the region, which are

---

[54] Hazans, Mihails (2013), "Emigration from Latvia: recent trends and economic impact", in OECD, *Coping with Emigration in Baltic and East East European Countries,* OECD Publishing. http://dx.doi.org/10.1787/9789264204928-7-en , p.4

[55] Hazans, Mihails (2013), "Emigration from Latvia: recent trends and economic impact", in OECD, *Coping with Emigration in Baltic and East East European Countries,* OECD Publishing. http://dx.doi.org/10.1787/9789264204928-7-en, p. 17

populated by the elderly and are essentially dying off. In many of these towns shops are closing due to lack of profits, so people have to rely only on mobile-shops that come several times per week bringing the essentials to sell. When I visited Daugavpils last summer, I was shocked: the second biggest city in the country was simply deserted and the people you could see were either primary school children or their grandparents, since the rest of the population emigrated to work (some of them took their families with them, some, especially single-mothers, work abroad and send money to remaining family members).

During the crisis, many people who all of a sudden became unemployed started working as self-employed, or free-lance, professionals or organizing small enterprises to survive. In Riga and more developed regions of Kurzeme and Vidzeme, these factors allowed people to earn money and the economy to not completely stagnate. In Latgale, however, the number of SMEs registered from 2008 is two times lower than in the rest of the country[56]. The difference in social-economic development of Latvian regions was further widened by the European sanctions towards the Russian Federation: Latgales machinery, wood, and food production was mostly working on exports to Russia, which had to be stopped, thus creating even more unemployment and lower standards of living. Further growing unemployment, historical cultural traditions varying from Latvian ones, proximity to Russia, recent events in Ukraine and particularly in Crimea, made Latgale a Latvian headache. The population of Latvia fears that the region that speaks Russian, and has more non-citizens than any other region in Latvia, will fall into the hands of Russian propaganda and provocation. There were already cases when the state security police had to investigate the spread of leaflets promoting accession to Russia[57], comparing Latgale to Crimea.

---

[56] Latvian Regions Development Agency, http://www.latreg.lv/pub/?lapa=81&oid=97
[57] LTV news program "Panorama" from 14.09.2014, http://www.tvnet.lv/zinas/latvija/526522-krievu_savienibas_reklama_latgali_pielidzina_krimai

So, to re-cap: we have a poor region with high unemployment rates that is dramatically depopulated already, and losing more working-age population to emigration; it is further stricken with the socio-economic effects of the EU sanctions, and faces potential political provocations from Russia.

One of the reasons why people emigrate is the loss of jobs, and hence lack of opportunity to live a decent and respected life. What do regional authorities in Latgale and Latvian government do to improve this situation? Paradoxically, the answer would be – nothing. Latvia mentions growth and employment[58] as its priorities during the EU Presidency; however it does nothing to promote them at home. The region saw the renovation of schools and cultural objectives; construction of social sites like swimming pools or educational centers, huge concert halls, and a bigger renovation of a highway, all done in cooperation with European Regional Development Fund, European Social Fund, and Cohesion Fund. Of course, one can argue that creating infrastructure is important to attract investors or even start a successful business. True. However, the development of infrastructure should be paralleled with monetary and fiscal policies aimed at creating jobs, which isn't happening.

As we have established earlier, SMEs in Latgale are less developed than in other Latvian regions. The rise of SMEs during the crisis was possible due to the innovative tax rate of 9% for businesses employing 5 or less people, introduced by the Latvian government to allow people to work as self-employed and not go into the shadow economy of, "salaries in the envelopes". Even this revolutionary measure didn't help Latgale; this year the government decided to increase the tax rate to 11% with the idea of further increasing it to 15% by 2017, which surely will not help develop local small businesses. Factories all over Latvia are closing down or slowing down its production due to European sanctions

---

[58] Latvian Presidency of the Council of the European Union website, https://eu2015.lv/the-presidency-and-eu/trio-presidency

towards Russia - this has especially influenced Latgale. However, instead of supporting business, for example by introducing a 0% tax rate on business profits that are invested back into production, like in Estonia, or lowering taxes in general to support business, the government advice is to ask for compensation from the EU for the losses due to sanctions, thus creating a stronger dependence on European funds. Latvian government adds changes to the taxation system at least once in two years, which makes it unpredictable and doesn't help attract investors who could help develop production in the region. All these measures and positions will not improve the situation in Latgale, but will only stimulate further emigration from the region.

Latgale is a Latvian region with a sad history of high emigration and deteriorating socio-economic conditions. High reliance on European Funds will not help solve this problem. Only fiscal and monetary policies aimed at boosting SMEs and business in general can help create jobs, improve the economy, and make people willing to stay there. At the moment the Latvian government is not doing enough; the latest results of polling show that 9%[59] of the population aged between 18 and 65 plan to leave the country to improve their material status, and 17% do not exclude such an opportunity. All of these do not leave much room for positive takes on regional disparity, and leave the case of Latgale in a morbid perspective.

---

[59] Hazans, Mihails (2013), "Emigration from Latvia: recent trends and economic impact", in OECD, *Coping with Emigration in Baltic and East East European Countries,* OECD Publishing. http://dx.doi.org/10.1787/9789264204928-7-en,p. 28

# JUSTYNA MICHALIK
## - Regional disparities: Poland in Europe, Poland vs. Europe

Since 2014 the European Union consists of 28 countries with different histories, cultures, economic performance, and around 507 000 000 inhabitants.[60] The enlargement process in the last 11 years, which led to the incorporation of the Eastern European countries, made the regional disparities even stronger than before. The European Commission has proposed a division of the EU-25 into four clusters to present the main differences between the EU regions and underline the most important factors which determine disparities.

In the first cluster we found 117 regions mostly from Northern and Central Europe (and 2 regions from Estonia and Hungary), which represented around 43% of the EU-25 population and territory. Their main characteristics were low unemployment, wide offering of services, a modern, mostly urban economy and an active population with higher education levels. The second cluster consisted of 31 regions and almost half of them were capital regions of older and newer EU countries – Vienna, Brussels, Berlin, and Prague, for example. They comprised 16% of the EU-25 population and only 3% of the total geographic area. Regions of this cluster were also wealthy, with education and unemployment levels a bit below the average. In the third cluster 51 regions of convergence from Southern Europe were included – with lower levels of the economic factors, higher education and higher unemployment levels than the EU average – which represented around 21% of the population and territory. The fourth cluster consisted of the eastern convergence regions with the highest unemployment, economic factors below the average and high

---

[60]http://ec.europa.eu/eurostat/tgm/table.do?tab=table&init=1&language=en&pcode=tps00001&plugin=1, Eurostat, *Table Population on 1 January*, 2014

education levels. Poland was ranked among the countries in the fourth cluster.[61]

The regional disparities in Europe were also visible from the Eurostat data ("Gross domestic product (GDP) per inhabitant, purchasing power standard (PPS), by NUTS 2 regions (% of the EU average, EU = 100)"). The best performing regions (from 125-348 of the EU average) were located mainly in the central and northern European countries (the western part of Germany, the Nordics, Austria, Northern Italy), whereas the lowest values (19-50) characterised the eastern regions of Poland, Romania and Bulgaria. Masovia (Polish capital city region) was situated amongst the second wealthiest regions with 107 in 2011. In the two best groups the capital cities of the Czech Republic, Slovakia and Romania, were also present, as well as the central region of Hungary.[62]

In another typology – according to the attractiveness of the region to migrants and visitors 2001 – 2007 – Poland was present in the first and second class (out of four classes). The first class was comprised of 54 EU regions with net emigration and the second class encompassed 202 EU regions with slightly positive net immigration rates and net visitation rates rather greater than in the first class. In the third and fourth classes mostly ranked regions of older EU member states with higher rates. In Poland, similar to some other capitals of Central – Eastern Europe might have been observed the on-going relative attractiveness of the Warsaw region which concentrated job opportunities and other important economic factors.[63]

---

[61] http://aei.pitt.edu/9029/1/DelCampo.pdf, C. Del Campo, C.M.F. Monteiro, J. Oliveira Soares, CES, Working Paper Series 131, *The Socioeconomic Diversity of European Regions*, 2006, p. 11-13.

[62] http://ec.europa.eu/eurostat/web/regions/statistics-illustrated, Eurostat, *Gross domestic product (GDP) per inhabitant, in purchasing power standard (PPS), by NUTS 2 regions (% of the EU average, EU = 100)*, 2011

[63] http://www.espon.eu/main/Menu_Publications/Menu_MapsOfTheMonth/map1203.html, ESPON,

The problem of the labour market's concentration in Warsaw and the surrounding area was presented in other publications as well. According to the Central Economic Information Centre 354593 companies were set up in 2013 and 343214 (around 307 000 individual entities and around 36 000 registered ones) in 2014. Almost 13 000 were registered in the Masovian voivodeship, around 4 500 in Greater Poland, around 3000 – 3500 in each 3 southern voivodeships (Silesian, Lesser Poland and Lower Silesian). By comparison, in 3 eastern voivodeships only around 2500 companies were registered in 2014 altogether. Around 33% of the all new individual entities in 2014 were set up in the Masovian, Silesian and Greater Poland voivodeships.[64] Moreover, around 550 among 1600 international investments in 2014 were companies located in Warsaw. New international companies to Poland in 2013 came mainly from Germany (348), The Netherlands (134), France (131), the United Kingdom (96), Italy (80) and from the USA (173).[65] In comparison to other European cities – for instance Frankfurt and Munich – it might have been observed that Warsaw, Bucharest and Prague had raised their position in the world city network of global services.[66]

This is only a small amount of data that shows the regional disparities within the country are of great importance to Warsaw and for the Polish labour market. Despite the huge absorption of the EU funds since 2004 and great improvements in the infrastructure of the eastern Polish regions (by the end of November 2013, Polish beneficiaries of ESI funds spent 61% of the allocated funds, moreover around 92,000 contracts were signed, which was around 92% of the total allocations for Poland[67]), the

---

Attractiveness of Regions to Migrants and Visitors, 2012
[64] http://www.coig.com.pl/nowe-firmy-w-polsce_2014_2013.php, Centralny Ośrodek Informacji Gospodarczej
[65] http://www.paiz.gov.pl/publikacje/inwestorzy_zagraniczni_w_polsce#, PAIiIZ, *List of Major Foreign Investors in Poland - December 2013*
[66]http://www.espon.eu/main/Menu_Publications/Menu_MapsOfTheMonth/map120 2.html, ESPON, *Evolution of cities servicing global capital*, 2012
[67] http://insideurope.eu/node/487, Biuletyn Informacyjny Nr. 32, *Absorption Rates*

differences between the capital city and a few other major cities versus, especially, the eastern provinces are still visible. The EU funds will preserve their importance for these regions but the question is what other measures should be taken by the government and local administration in order to attract tourism and international investors and reduce the disparities.

The main problems in the Polish provinces could be the lower chances for significant progress in terms of economic growth, fighting unemployment and/or attracting tourism. The key factors involved in solving them are not only direct investments or long term supporting funds, but also a kind of mentality change, in particular creating an entrepreneurial spirit, helping to develop natural skills and adjusting education programmes to the demands of the market. Here, the role of the regional administration and local organisations of different origins (social, religious, political, etc.) could be crucial. They could encourage people to create their own space in the market, implement bold and fresh ideas into the local environment and to actively search for sponsors and supporters of their goals. Moreover, they may present a more appropriate and flexible approach because of the limited number of citizens under their patronage, and a deeper understanding of the particular areas where the actions should be taken.

Of course, the role of the state administration in financial support, providing access to education and adjusting the labour force capabilities within the current economic situation should not be underestimated. However, such problems as incorrect distribution and allocation of state or international funds, inefficient or insufficient changes in education system (e.g. introducing obligatory traineeships for students that should help them to prepare better for their professional life but are usually perceived as an unnecessarily and additional ballast in an overloaded university programme) or difficulties with creating job opportunities can be resolved only through proper cooperation between administration units at different levels, non –

governmental organisations and representatives of the private sector. Only complex knowledge and actions combined with particular, ad hoc activities can result in long-term changes that could decrease the differences between the capital/ economic/ cultural centres and the provinces.

It is certain that economic development will play an even greater role in overcoming the differences in Poland. Thanks to the EU Funds, international investments and high human potential (the number of inhabitants of a productive age and the quantity of people with higher education) there is a chance to continue reducing the disparities. However, without a wise government policy in terms of supporting families, creating new job opportunities and developing a sustainable economy, Poland might face demographic and ecological problems that will only deepen current regional differences.

# KEITH HENRY
# - Using Agenda 21 to Address Regional Disparities

Since the 1992 Earth Summit in Rio de Janeiro, sustainable development has been put to the fore by politicians, policy makers and local activists. Sustainable development incorporates more than just awareness of the scarcity of resources and the impact for future generations. It includes social equity and citizen empowerment to develop for their own needs (Evans and Theobald, 2003). Agenda 21 and its spin off Local Agenda 21 action plans aimed to address this need for people deciding and developing for themselves. Much study has delved into how different nations or global regions have addressed this global consensus to embrace sustainable development practices.

In order to address regional disparities it is important to look at who are the key stakeholders in helping these regions tackle their differences. As someone who has been a member of different community organisations who attempted to generate local growth I have seen the abuse of programmes such as LEADER funding first hand but I have also seen what benefit they can have when controlled and monitored appropriately. This paper outlines how Local Agenda 21 has been implemented in Ireland to help address regional disparities and evaluates the European response to help address regional differences.

## Sustainable Development and Local Agenda 21:

A great deal of the literature I have examined has emphasised that while there is a need for sustainable planning and development frameworks for the future, much of the language and initiatives included the in documents is little more than rhetoric. Scholars such as Clark and Netherwood (1999) and Parker and Keating (2006) agree that the Local Agenda is an almost hypocritical document insofar as it wishes to seek bottom up decision making, yet it is pushing this reform agenda on authorities for enactment. They are cynical and sceptical of politics generally in its attempt to reform itself to develop sustainably. They put forward the notion that the reform proposals are an attempt to cover up the faults and failures of politics and appease an ever burgeoning number of community groups intent on having a say (Clark and Netherwood, 1999),(Keating, 2006). Therefore rather than politicians wishing to sustainably develop, they are sustaining their role within development but opening up the process to give the appearance of inclusive and collaborative decision making.

Arguments have also been put forward on how to incorporate sustainable development into societies. Parker and Selman (1999) go against the grain of most debates on Local Agenda and sustainable development and argue for more monetary and legislative initiatives to address sustainable development. They claim that encouraging civicness and participation is a copout solution. As contrasting as their work is to other academics, the argument that those who are pushing the reforms are attempting to spread the blame for bad practice for self sustaining purposes is also expressed. At the other end of the spectrum, Clark and Netherwood (1999) from their study in Wales, propose that there are already voluntary groups working in communities to foster sustainable practices. These groups are working outside the political system and are proving successful and therefore the connotation that Local Agenda reforms will kick start community involvement and consciousness of sustainability is weakened, as they are already doing the work. However one could counter argue that this is not the case in every locality and rather than Local Agenda wishing to take over the good work of established voluntary groups, it wishes to encourage the spread of such groups and use them as examples of how people can empower themselves.

**A Case for Europe:**

A number of academics have studied the results of, or developed their own survey based on the Local Authorities Self Assessment on the Local Agenda (LASALA) study by the ICELI, a body promoting sustainable governance in urban centres. Joas and Grönholm (2004) analyse the results through regionalising the data and found that the Nordic nations are the best performers. They maintain that this comes as no great shock as there has been a long tradition of participatory governance in the region. While they find that most "western" nations perform the best overall, cities in the former Soviet nations that participated in the self assessment perform very well in generating awareness and committing to Local Agenda. This may reflect a strong desire to become part of "western Europe" or perhaps represent a lacklustre committal by these so called western nations to an agenda they are not enthused about.

Evans and Theobald (2010) also use LASALA data to evaluate the state of Local Agenda integration and how cities and nations should be performing. This study along with Joas and Grönholm (2004) and (Ansell and Gash, 2008), all agree that local authorities in Europe are still reluctant to open up decision making processes and that commitment and enthusiasm has dwindled. What was evident from these studies is an uneven response to Local Agenda among and within regions. Its implementation was often left in the hands of a small group of individuals or indeed one individual within a local authority. This is an interesting concept as perhaps the lack of action on sustainable development practices is a result of an undesirability to take on the task of encouraging communities and policy makers to embrace it. The costs of implementing and training staff is also briefly commented on but unfortunately does not take into account the recent economic downturn across the continent.

**Participation and Governance:**

Agenda 21 emphasises the need for communities to become involved in decision making for developing their areas and recommends that local authorities open up the board rooms to allow this to take place. However, this desire for openness and transparency was not welcomed by many, as research of the literature proves. Callanan (2005), Mullally (2001) and Parker and Selman (1999), all comment on the reluctance of civil servants within local authorities to have their role in local development reviewed. The perceived loss of status and authority in having their plans and proposals put before collaborative governance structures was a sore point. Many viewed reform as an indication that higher authorities believed they were not doing their job adequately.

Similarly for politicians who enact development projects and proposals, there was a feeling of a loss of power to decide on behalf of the people they represent. Callanan (2005) puts forward an interesting observation in the lack of accountability for non-elected stakeholders being a divisive issue among the paid officials and the publically elected politicians. It was also found that scepticism and suspicion existed about what agendas stakeholders may have (Parker and Selman, 1999), (Evans and Theobald, 2010). Rather than encourage good relationships between community representatives and policy makers, Local Agenda in these instances has done the opposite.

It has been argued that community groups should lead the change in their localities and be involved in the political process (Pike et.al, 2006), (Ansell and Gash 2008). However Keating (2006) states while this may be the aspiration, within new participatory bodies decision making is controlled by a certain elite. A relevant argument to the dissertation, it generates questions as to who actually is representing the community within these participatory boards and are marginalised groups excluded (Considine and Giguere, 2009). Questions such as might they be the same individuals on all such boards and how or who elected them to be the voice of the community come to mind. Considering this argument, looking at the mechanism at which decisions are reached within participatory bodies and who makes up the board becomes significant.

Much of the literature currently discussed has briefly addressed that Local Agenda is a top down initiative to encourage bottom up development. This appears to be a contradictory method to achieving a desired change. It is evident from the reading that across the continent there is a weak system of local government (Ansell and Gash, 2008), (Considine and Giguere, 2009), (Mullally, 2001). Local authorities take their lead from regional or national government policy while European governments react to changes within the EU or international agreements. Much of the initiatives promoted by the EU are made attractive for national and regional governments by associating them with funding as evident in the schemes such as REPS or LEADER (Woods, 2005).
Furthermore, Parker and Selman (1999) suggest that communities are more receptive to local authority policy changes than national ones. Yet if national governments are cognisant of this, they may manipulate their hold over local government and push an agenda upon them and give the appearance of local consent. This is a very relevant argument for the dissertation as well as for current local government reform and financing.

With collaborative participatory decision making comes collaborative blame when developments go wrong. The literature has suggested that stakeholders are often reluctant or sceptical of inclusive bodies as these also offer the ability to spread or pass the blame to others (Callanan, 2005). Academics believe that partnership projects are often treated in a patronising manner by officials who see it as a means of appeasing individuals and groups. They also believe that the relatively short political cycles of 4-5 years mean that little long term progress can be made (Considine and Giguere, 2009).

## Local Agenda in Ireland:

As with most other European nations, Ireland took its direction on Local Agenda from Brussels. The Guidelines on Local Agenda 21 produced by the government state that local authorities are most closely associated and best placed for local development planning (Department of Environment, 2001). It referred to the position of county councillors in the Local Government Act 1991 as decision makers on behalf of the people they represent, yet it also proposed that councils should be facilitators for planning discussions by the whole community. It identified sustainable development as the key priority of local and national government, development that would tackle the inequalities within Irish society as well as promote enterprise and transport improvements (Department of Environment, 2001).

Partnerships were signalled as ways of including the community in local development projects. Callanan (2005) outlines how Special Policy Committees have great potential for more inclusive democracy but they are hindered by the inability to keep focus. He agrees with similar theories proposed by scholars such as Evans and Theobald (2010), that participatory bodies are often forums for pushing stakeholder agendas. This is an important observation which the dissertation investigates.

Ireland appears to have the same challenges as Europe in terms of weak local government that is reliant on national direction. Gaynor (2009), Mullally (2001) and Callanan (2005) all agree that Local Agenda in Ireland is a top down directed initiative. However Moseley et al (2001) does not agree and based on their research of 19 partnership groups, it was local individuals that were the key drivers of participatory governance. This differing research provides a number of considerations for investigation in the dissertation such as if there are individuals encouraging participatory governance and are these an exclusive group of self appointed leaders that Keating (2006) refers to, or true representatives of a body of people intent on contributing to the development of their area. Mullally (2001) in his research into local authorities, found that staff training was the first priority for local authorities before public engagement. This would suggest that a certain amount of staff within a local authority were responsible for the implementation of Local Agenda. If this was the case then it is important to assess if the training this person/s received was filtered into other departments within the local authorities or left the sole responsibility of one person or a group of people.

The reforms encouraged by the government through its various policy documents and legislative arrangements, has not resulted in sustainable planning according to Gaynor (2009). In this article she hits out at the bad planning decisions that resulted in an economic crash. The excessive re-zoning of land, developing of housing estates in illogical locations and vastness of empty retail units bring local authorities and their associated participatory frameworks in for great criticism. She along with Moseley et.al (2001) maintain that the focus of many partnerships has been on economics and employment rather than sustainable development and that similar to Callanan's argument they have lost their focus.

## Conclusion:

There is a growing awareness that regional disparities need to be addressed across Europe as a whole and within individual nations. The response to this problem has seen governments attempt to democratise the decision making process so that local people can shape their own future as they know the problems of their area best. However this system of returning power to the grassroots has and can be abused by both governments and citizens. I have been involved in several committees which have been created as spin offs from the Agenda 21 reforms and their sole intention has been to get as much funding as possible from projects such as LEADER and then find a way to spend it. Long term planning and sustainable development is not something many of these groups engage with. While having great sports facilities in a small rural area is a great amenity it is of little use if there is almost 20% unemployment. A more streamlined method of providing funding for community groups to address regional disparities is needed. Indeed the disparities between regions across the EU have been replicated at a micro level within national counties/districts as a result of these new initiatives such as LEADER and Local Agenda 21. At a local level certain sectors of society benefit more from this bottom up development as they have a better human resource skill set to work from and therefore are better experienced in applying for funding.

In essence the move to democratise the decision process for balanced regional development is a positive one. However it is foolish to expect that local groups can solve things on their own. There needs to be an agreed direction and goal that local groups and governments are working to in order to make their region more competitive. Through sharing of ideas members across Europe can draw contrasts and similarities as to what worked for them and what didn't. A one size fits all approach will not work as each region has its own unique assets and limits be they physical, human, economic or other after all that is how we decide where one region ends and another begins. In Ireland's case the Economic recovery is heavily centred in the Greater Dublin region. Groups in more rural parts have clutched onto the Local Agenda reforms and LEADER funding for over a decade and while facilities have improved and there is a greater awareness of local development, many areas are little better off than when they started. Therefore I would hope that this conference will recognise that while local citizens should be involved in tackling regional disparities there needs to be a discourse between political institutions and local groups to ensure that their efforts and resources are not fruitless in tackling the problem.

# MANEL MSALMI
## - Partnership Agreements and Trade and Growth in World Affairs, the Key Solution to a Healthy European Economy

The regional disparities in Europe show different economic inequalities and present different challenges for liberal leaders and youth. The European economy is a diversified one which depends on different factors such as localization, labour markets and economic developments. However, dealing with such an issue in Europe might be very complicated given that there are a lot of regional differences and different unemployment rates. This paper aims to show that partnership agreements and a European trade policy are the key elements that could fight against regional inequalities.

In effect, the Partnership agreements within the Cohesion Policy 2014-2020 aim at establishing operational programs within the EU and preparing an overview of the key issues of the different member states. Such a strategy can be beneficial in the sense that it establishes a dialogue between the member states and an exchange of the different issues that might differ from one country to another. Moreover, these operational programs can be fund-specific or multi-fund which in turn allows the member states to select their specific projects and priorities as well as their managing authorities. The cohesion policy allows a certain degree of independence and freedom to different member states in terms of financial, geographical and economic management. There is also a place for discussion, cooperation and dialogue between local and regional authorities in order to improve the partnership principle.

Trade policy based on cohesion between the different member states goes beyond the ordinary and the conventional trade agreements to focus on development and the improvement of the socio-economic status of certain regions together with boosting local economies and stimulating growth as well as sharing equal opportunities in Europe and worldwide. As a matter of fact, the European Partnership agreement can be a starting point to boost regional integration and raise competitiveness between the different regions. Competitiveness can create in turn a kind of individual expertise given that each partner can be a leader in his project and benefit from the skills and experience of the other showing equal distribution of management skills, profits and losses. Finally these kinds of agreement help create equal job opportunities in the different regions and attract skilled candidates who are eager to move from one region to another and invest in disadvantaged areas.

The second focal point would be Trade liberalization which is in my view one of the most important factors that can boost the European Union's economy. In fact, international trade helps creating jobs and achieving growth in difficult economic circumstances. Economic growth depends on operating on both supply and demand, trade is an efficient tool to boost the economy given that Europe is well placed to benefit from international trade. The EU economy, with the rise of new competitors, can benefit much more from globalization. Despite the economic and financial crisis, Europe is still an attractive place for foreign investment because of its strategic placement .In fact; Europe remains the largest recipient of international investment and one of the largest creators of job opportunities in the world. Even though member states can differ in terms of competitiveness, the rapid development of regional and global investment can be a motif to a have a change in trade policymaking. Developing the theory of open economies would allow disadvantaged economies to grow faster, be more effective and give EU consumers a variety of goods and products at lower prices. Europe's focus on foreign investment together with its openness to the global market would enable European firms to enlarge their business and invest abroad by creating jobs in Europe and elsewhere. Global trade and investment is definitely a golden opportunity for Europe to reach global markets and to create more jobs and goods and services at lower prices. The idea of opening trade could be very beneficial in the sense that it creates economic growth, consumer benefits and more job opportunities as well as better paid jobs in a global and competitive economy. It is true that such a policy has a lot of challenges but it enhances regulatory cooperation, supports green growth between the different member states as well as sustainable development.

To conclude, partnership agreements as well as trade and investments are one of the key solutions that enable Europe to fight against disparities between the different member states by creating a liberal market, cooperation and investment and economic growth within the European sphere and the global market on equal footing.

**References:**
-European Parliamentary Research service: Partnership Agreements within Cohesion Policy 2014-2020
-Trade, Growth and Jobs: Commission Contribution to the European Council

# MAXIMILIAN HEILMANN
## - European Future: Cooperation and collaboration for a growing European economy

The financial debit crisis showed us how the world economy can influence the local markets. Many factors are connected with economic growth. Several are obvious and well known, but there are also other factors that can have an influence. These are related to infrastructure and the educational System.

In the year 2015 several countries within the European Union are still struggling with economic problems. In the global economy it is not only important to have the infrastructure and capability for production and trade. Moreover, each country's position towards global business is important. The European States can only operate as a global player if they cooperate with each other and set goals together, in order to reach the same level as China, the USA and India. With such a future plan we can reach one important goal: to be one European player in the global market.

Furthermore, we should open the member states to more markets and use trading agreements in this context from our member states to extend them to all member states of the European Union. Especially the German businesses are able to create opportunities or open the local market for the German companies with AHK offices abroad. The AHK is a partner organization of the German industry association IHK and represents the interests of German industry abroad. This institution has over the last couple years created a good network with the local businesses and got access to trade for Germany.

From my point of view this is a very good example of how business can work, without intervention from the national parliaments. One part of the solution to get back to a positive growth in the long term is to use such institutions like the AHK and extend their rights, and create a general framework to support the inventions of European companies in other counties to get access to this market.

Beside the investments of European companies in the markets of foreign countries, it is nevertheless important to further open the European market to foreign investors. Until now there are still barriers, even for European companies who want to invest within the European Union.

Another important point is how member states invest their capital. A question that arises here is how low the taxes can be in order to cover the expenses of a state (Medicare, Social benefits, subsidies and so on). High taxes can be a reason for companies to reduce their investments. Less labour and higher unemployment is just one result. Investments should be easier if we are to create a positive growth in Europe.

The European Union was originally just an economic union. Nowadays we are one society with shared responsibilities, including social and economic welfare for each member state. It is time to learn from each other's strengths. Cooperation and collaboration is another goal which we have to focus on. In the economic sector there is still a lot of potential to work together. Finally, it is important to act as one player in the global market. Otherwise it is difficult to gain acceptance as a global player alongside Russia, China and the USA. Therefore, the European Union should coordinate the representative offices of each member state. This would lead to more acceptance abroad. Moreover, this would bring the companies of the European Union a larger influence on the regional markets.

Extended markets can open opportunities for European companies that currently have problems selling their products in local markets. Such opportunities can create international business. Not only does this benefit the operating company, it additionally gives the market for labour a larger diversity.

As already mentioned, there are investments necessary to create economic growth. Beside private investments, investments from the European Union are also important. A good infrastructure (Streets, Railway, Airport and Internet) can not only create opportunities for companies, it helps companies to extend their range of customers. It is one responsibility of the European Union. Especially for regions with a high unemployment rate, such a subsidy can create positive effects on the labor market and for the economic growth of the EU as a whole. The EU can be successful, and can interact as a global player, because the economic success is sustainable. The long-term perspective is of great importance here.

Companies play a major role in the economic success, but it should not go unmentioned that the mobility of workers can help to reduce skilled shortages. The freedom of movement for workers is a step in the right direction. Based on the statutes of Article 45 TFEU (ex 39 and 48) the mobility is guaranteed. Now it is easier to get skilled workers from abroad to a local company to extend their business. It creates possibilities for investments into human capital. Human capital is connected to education. There is no other capital that is more important for the European Union than human capital, because the member States can never mine like Russia, the USA or China does. The EU does business with the creativity and innovation of the work force. Nowhere else is education so well-known than in Europe.

Business formation and entrepreneurship is the foundation for the success of the European economy. Only with new ideas can it be possible to create economic growth. The European Union can use innovation, productivity and effectivity to get back into the global market as a global player.

To conclude is to say this: the economic growth rate is related to many factors, but it is possible to stimulate the economy to get back to a positive growth rate for the whole European Union. Opportunities are given by the national parliaments and regional investors or companies can use them. With these aspects the European Union can interact together and play a different role in the world in the future.

Focussing on all of these aspects it is possible to get back into business with good prospects for success.

# SID LUKKASSEN
# - Europe: a Path Towards All Your Innovative Needs

"In ten, twenty, fifty years time, people will look back at the decisions we took today. Think of the questions they will ask. Did Europe in 2012 respond to digital realities? Did we enable, anticipate and adapt to disruptive change? Did we cooperate and remove barriers to innovation? Did we compete on the global stage? In short: Were we ready to ready to welcome and usher in a new economic reality? Or did we carry on doing everything the same, and got caught unprepared?"
– Neelie Kroes, Vice-President of the European Commission responsible for the Digital Agenda, June 21, 2012

In this treatise we will be examining the innovation policy of the European Union, comparing it to that of the United States. It has been said by Neelie Kroes that ten years ago, the top ten ranking of most competitive companies on a global scale was dominated by European enterprises, whereas today, that list is dominated by American businesses. Most innovation, considering the past ten years, has taken place in the ICT sector, and thus the question becomes what European businesses can do to be more innovative than they are right now. It seems we have not been as innovative, economically speaking, as our North-Atlantic counterparts.

This treatise will be built-up in six sections. In the first section the current picture will be painted. It will turn out this picture is not a clear-cut black and white – we shall explain the situation by reflecting upon the elements involved in measurement. Secondly, we will clarify what the European Union is doing by elucidating the digital agenda and the flagship. Thirdly, we will draw a more direct comparison between entrepreneurial culture in Europe and the United States, and after that provide suggestions concerning entrepreneurial competitiveness and re-launching industry. Before going on to the conclusion, we shall analyse these findings through the scope of ALDE. How can liberal principles be involved in working towards future results?

## 1. The current picture

The Global Innovation Index is a massive report published by Insead, an international business school, and the World Intellectual Property Organization, an agency of the United Nations. When looking at the Global Innovation Index rankings of 2012, it quickly becomes apparent that the United States takes the lead over Europe with companies such as Google, Microsoft and Apple. Europe, however, has Skype and a number of high performing German car companies. Still it remains clear that European enterprise has not been able to capitalize on the digital revolution the way that business in the United States has.

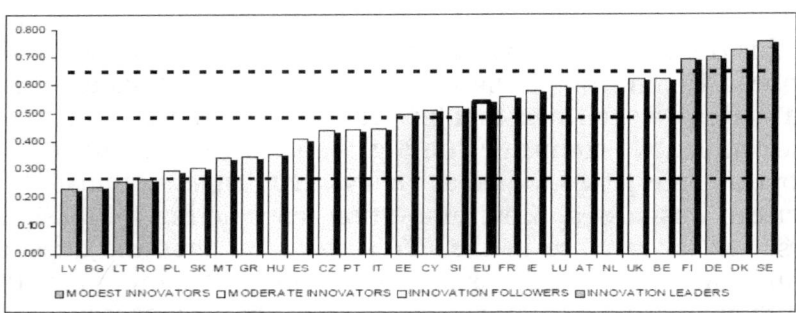

**Figure 1.** EU member states innovation performance, based on Innovation Union scoreboard, 2011. *Source:* Innovation Union Scoreboard, 2012

EU member states can be grouped into 4 performance groups:
- Innovation leaders - Denmark, Finland, Germany and Sweden
- Innovation followers - Austria, Belgium, Cyprus, Estonia, France, Ireland, Luxembourg, Netherlands, Slovenia and the UK

- Moderate innovators - Czech Republic, Greece, Hungary, Italy, Malta, Poland, Portugal, Slovakia and Spain
- Modest innovators - Bulgaria, Latvia, Lithuania and Romania

What makes this picture more interesting, however, is that the United States is still outperformed on the Global Innovation Index rankings by Switzerland, Sweden, Finland, the United Kingdom, Netherlands, Denmark and Ireland. This, of course, is part of the fact that the European Union is constructed from nations with many different types of economies. It explains why Europe, as a whole, is as of yet less innovative than the United States. Therefore, one might argue that the global economic arena is not so much Europe versus the United States, as it is the United States *and* Europe versus the BRICS, meaning Brazil, Russia, India, China and South Africa. Obviously, it is true that the more wealthy the inhabitants of BRICS countries become, the more interesting those countries become as markets to us, due to the purchasing power of consumers. Yet we live in a world where there is a scarcity of resources; meaning that it will become tougher to maintain a high standard of living if those resources have to be shared.

Another question is whether the earth can even sustain the development of BRICS countries to Western standards of consumption and production. What does this scarcity of resources mean for the Western world, which is outsourcing most of its direct production (*maakindustrie*) to nations where manual labour is cheap and plentiful? What is the value of Western currency, tied up with service-based economies, in a world where every geopolitical entity will try to grab hold of resources to safeguard its future developments? Not to mention the impact of the average human being's footprint in combination with the overpopulation. These questions obviously require a geopolitical approach, and cannot be answered with the common capitalistic mindset. An entrepreneur needs to see profit within ten years or perhaps fifteen years at most. To tackle the aforementioned conundrums we need vision and philosophy. We need to be prepared to look decades ahead into the future, and comprehend the different civilizations and the way their empires develop. Just take a glance at China, be marvelled by the intensity of the effort they muster, and the speed at which they are getting their energy production up.

To gauge the implication of the Global Development Index, however, we must remark that what we define as "Development" stands and falls with the way it is measured. The Global Development Index takes into account human resources, excellence in research systems, finance and support, firm investments, linkages and entrepreneurship, intellectual assets, innovators, and economic effects. More specifically, the Index looks at new doctorate graduates, the percentage of the population having completed tertiary education, international scientific publications, public spending on Research and Development, patents, export of medium and high-tech products, knowledge intensive service export and the revenues from licenses and patents abroad.

The Index describes that both the United States and Japanese performance is well above that of the EU28.[68] The EU28 has, however, a strong lead compared to each of the BRIC countries. The performance lead over India has remained stable over the last 5 years and has slightly increased over Russia. China and Brazil are both catching up towards the EU28 where the rate of Brazil is more modest than China's. The United States is performing better than the EU28 except when it comes to the export of knowledge intensive services. It has increased its lead in new doctorate degrees, international co-publications, business R&D expenditure and license and patent revenues. The lead in tertiary education has, however, decreased. Out of 143 nations ranked in 2014, Insead noticed, "spectacular progress for Russia moving up 13 places to 49$^{th}$ and China, moving up by 6 places to reach 29$^{th}$, which makes

---

[68] The economic and population size of the United States, Japan and the BRICS outweighs those of the individual European Union Member States and it therefore makes more sense to compare these countries with the aggregate of the EU28.

China comparable to many high-income economies. India slipped 10 places to 76th."[69]

Japan has increased its lead in performance and excellence overall, except that European scientific articles are much more cited than Japanese ones, and the EU28 has more new doctorate degrees. In knowledge intensive services exports India and Brazil are performing better than the EU28. Overall there is a clear performance lead in favour of Europe, but this lead is decreasing, as Brazil's innovation performance has grown at a faster rate than of the EU28. The same goes for India and China, and for China it goes that there is a performance lead in the export of medium and high-tech products. In comparison to Russia there is a clear lead for the EU28, and this lead is increasing. When it comes to new doctorate degrees and tertiary education Russia is, however, performing better.

When it comes to international competitiveness, the European Union is the major World trader. In 2010, its export accounted for 17% of World export value of goods and services, and import – for 17.5 % of World import value. Although, the rapid economic growth and increasing involvement in global trade of the BRICS players is sometimes perceived as a threat to economic position of the European Union, the European Union export share remains stable over the years bearing some slight changes. This might be said to demonstrate the success of the European Union foreign trade policies and high competitiveness of the European Union economy as the whole. According to the European Commission (2010), in the last decade the European Union succeeded in increasing the share of high-tech products in international trade, while the United States and Japan lost some of these shares to China's increase. In 2007, the European Union export of high-tech products accounted for 16.9% of the World shares, following China, which in the same year took a 21.2% share, and the United States took 13.7%.

---

[69] Bruno Lanvin 'The World's Most Innovative Countries 2014' (July 17, 2014).

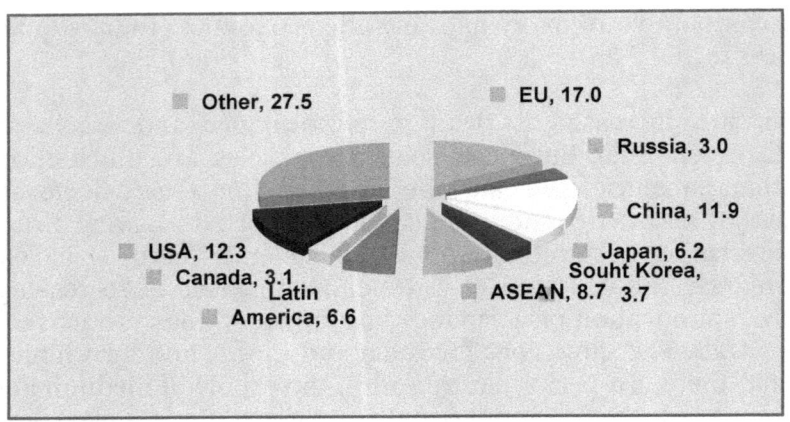

**Figure 2.** Export shares of goods and services, worldwide, in 2010, in %
*Source*: Angele Kedaitiene, based on the data from European Commission, 2012

We have to talk a bit about the cultural circumstances that form the bedding of these competitive and innovative performances. Generally speaking, the better the rule of law the better the innovation, but this is not necessarily true for Russia. Due to differing views on copyrights and contracts, China is copying a lot of the technologies that are developed elsewhere. This means that a less inventive company can be more innovative depending on your standards. Thus the commonly held adage, that innovation is greater where ideas can circulate within a society more freely, is not necessarily true. Applestore is located in China while Bengalore is a capital city in India and a very important centre of information technology. These areas are pools of excellence and productivity, with little to no regulations and cheap labour. The workforce is younger as well. Insead noticed that "among the leading countries, education has become a lifelong pursuit, from learning on the job and in a university, a multidisciplinary system of education from the early stages is encouraged, where silos cease to exist and ideas can be shared across disciplines." It was also noted that fluid labor markets accelerate innovation and this is one area that continues to hold back Korea (16th) and Japan (21th).[70]

Taking a closer look at entrepreneurial culture proves that in the European Union, business is more timid about risk management. When it comes to venture capital, people are not eager to invest in science, and wait for funding to come from the government. In the United States there is a different attitude to newness: "Is it new? I want it first!" Thus the EU28 runs a race to be second: "Let someone do it first and if it works we will tag along." The whole system of the United States is built to benefit the best, the top-performing. Whereas Europe is reigned by a more socialist spirit, the concept that it is *society* that lifts the human being beyond animal existence and that it is thus also societies´ task to invest in culture as well as science and research. As a result, in the United States there is a more individualistic *winner takes all* mentality when it comes to business, which breeds competition: High peaks and deep valleys. In Europe, we take more account of society as a whole, and thus we take away from the top to fill up the valleys. This, by contrast, could be said to stimulate laziness. One might argue that China is successful while also being a very collectivistic society, which it is. Unlike Europe, however, Chinese labourers do not have many entitlements and the Chinese government is more willing to apply force and pressure to stimulate productivity.

The bottom line of this first section is that Europe is in urgent need of a wake-up call to ready itself regarding the rise of the BRICS.

## 2. EU2020: The digital agenda and the flagship

Spending on Research and Development diminishes as we move from the North-West to the South-East. Considering great disparity in the investment as well as the output of innovation across the European Union, the viability of R&D convergence can

---

[70] Bruno Lanvin 'The World's Most Innovative Countries 2014' (July 17, 2014).

be questioned. The EU2020 directive aims to bring up the Research and Development budget to 3% of the GDP for each Member State. At first glance, three things are obvious. Firstly, the difference in strength in business investment in research between countries of the Euro zone and the new Member States is vast. Secondly, a closer look at the amount of researchers employed lays bare the private R&D effort as the most vulnerable aspect. Thirdly, the number of signed patents per Member State depends on the diversity present within the industrial sector in that Member State – such diversity is missing for most of the new Member States.[71]

It was in response to these facts that the Council of Europe decided in 2002 that 3% of GDP should be allocated to R&D. It was also stipulated that two thirds of this has to come from private investment. To make the political reality more in accordance with this decision, the <u>European Commission launched the flagship</u> in 2010. These are seven initiatives bundled under the name of EU2020. "A European strategy for smart, sustainable growth," which will ultimately result in an "Innovation Union," which means to say a place where innovative ideas get translated into products and jobs.

*"Financing research is making knowledge out of money.*
*Innovation is making money out of knowledge."*

While Europe is good at doing scientific research and creating knowledge, it is less so at making sure this knowledge gets put into practice, which is called the "valley of death." Thus, the European industrial process, economy and society at large do not prosper as a result of European research as much as they could. This is because, considered from a geopolitical angle, the European commercial sector is lagging behind when it comes to investment in science as well as R&D. The society of the United States, by contrast, is more permeated by an entrepreneurial spirit closing

---

[71] For more information, see: http://www.swp-berlin.org/fileadmin/contents/products/arbeitspapiere/Research_and_Development_KS.pdf (accessed Tuesday November 14).

this gap. This in turn creates a dilemma for the liberal ideology: On the one hand one wants a free market and does not wish to meddle in private business. On the other hand one wishes to maintain the international economic advantage and this requires investment in research and development. We will return to this point in section three.

The seven directives of the flagship are:

1. Digital Agenda for Europe
2. Innovation Union
3. Youth on the move
4. Resource efficient Europe
5. An industry policy for the globalisation era
6. An agenda for new skills and jobs
7. European platform against poverty

Directives 1, 2 and 3 are united under the motto "smart growth." 4 and 5 together form "sustainable growth," while 6 and 7 go under the label of "inclusive growth."

The Digital Agenda for Europe is to be understood as "The aim to reboot Europe's economy and help Europe's citizens and businesses to get the most out of digital technologies."[72] The Information and Communications Technology (ICT) sector accounts for 5% of European GDP, and ICTs have contributed to approximately 50% of the growth in EU productivity. The digital agenda in turn contains 101 actions and 13 specific goals. Without going into too much detail, we can state here that the aim is creating a Single Digital Market to increase internet speed and accessibility. This will make the European market attractive to foreign enterprise, enhance digital literacy skills, and help out when it comes to tackling societal challenges, such as an aging population. Increasing the internet use of disabled people is also a goal. The entire EU should be covered by broadband internet in

---

[72] For more information, see: https://ec.europa.eu/digital-agenda/node/1584 (accessed Tuesday November 14).

2013. The amount of population that has never used internet is to be cut in half from 30% to 15% in 2015.

To increase the European Union's innovation capacity, the flagship is set up to endow young people with the skills to engage in a more technological world and compete on a level of globalisation. What we need is to attract more young people to careers in research. More output in science requires more human capital. As professor Anne Glover put it: "In Europe we may not have oil or gas, but we have what you have in your minds . . . And what we will be able to make of it one day."[73] Bottom line: Research, as a profession, must be more attractive.

How to do this? The number of researchers in the European Union was 1,5 million FTE in 2008. The number of researchers in the labour force was 6 per 1000 in 2008, compared to 9 in the US and 11 in Japan. The difference is due to a much lower share of researchers in the business sector: 46% of total researchers in the EU against 68% in Japan and 79% in the US. China doubled from 0.7 in 2000 to 1.4 in 2007. Europe needs one million additional research jobs, "hard core science," meaning mathematical physics and chemistry. Curricula will need to be adapted. At present there seems to be little interest among women to work in the technical branches.

The United States has the same issue with attracting qualified science, technology, engineering and mathematics (STEM) graduates – not enough students go into those fields of education. Aside from making it more affordable for students to attend university, it is hard to see what either the European Union or United States could do to increase STEM graduates. The limits of malleability to human nature suggest that most people may not be intelligent, motivated or interested enough to enter fields like engineering or scientific research. Obviously, we no longer live in the age of the Enlightenment where the West was at the peak of its geopolitical power and the majority of publications and main

---

[73] 18 October 2012 at the Star Strek Event at European Parliament.

discourse was about philosophical and scientific ideas. We have moved from an *aristocratic culture*, where a life devoted to the pursuit of knowledge and disclosing the mysteries of nature was held to be honourable for its own sake, to a *bourgeois culture*, where no thing can enter the main narrative without the question: "How does this make money, and what does this gain for the ordinary man?" In *Sources of the Self* the liberal philosopher Charles Taylor notes how an ethics of, 'rigorous reason' and, 'heroic contemplation' gradually made way for a mercantile ethos.[74] This becomes obvious when one observes how reluctant the European private sector is to invest in hardcore science, as opposed to private business in the rest of the industrialized world.

The Horizon2020 aims to raise the budget to 80 billion euro between 2014 and 2020. This is part of the CIP – Competitiveness & innovation Framework Programme. 24.598 million is to be invested in top research, meaning an increase in funding by 77% for very successful European companies. The ERC, European Research Council, aims to strengthen industrial leadership in innovation by investing 17.938 million and provide 31.748 million for societal challenges such as climate change and the aging population.

Horizon2020 comes with a set of three pillars, the first one of which is Excellent Science, meaning to support talented and creative individuals and opening up new fields with future emerging technologies. This is done by strengthening the foundations of R&D; basic research and frontier research. Researchers are provided with excellent training and development opportunities through the Marie Curie actions, which is a research fellowship programme designed to increase researcher mobility. Horizon2020 will invest in electronic infrastructure to ensure European research infrastructure is accessible to all researchers in the world. The first pillar means to provide excellent in fields where this is necessary to remain a leading power internationally.

---

[74] Charles Taylor, *Bronnen van het zelf*, (Rotterdam 2009) 63-4, 223, 388.

This is a more short-term objective than investing in those Member States that might be excellent in the long term.

A debate has been sparkled around this pillar concerning the topic "widening excellence." Meaning that some political groups have suggested taking funding away from what they consider "already privileged" groups, and transfering these funds to Member States whose infrastructure is lagging behind. The reply to this should be that, for instance, the Greek government must ensure circumstances which make it attractive to innovate, by tackling bureaucratic and legal obstacles. The Malawian inventor William Kamkwamba built his family an electricity-generating windmill from spare parts, working from rough plans he found in a library book. Liberals ought to emphasize that if this is possible in Africa, it is also possible in Greece. Subsidies often work like sleeping-pills; they come with very clearly defined terms of what one must do to obtain them. But once this is ascertained, there is no further drive for optimization. The consequence is that people will stop looking ahead. This became clear in the Netherlands, where there were subsidies for solar panels. The consumers waited for the companies to receive the subsidies, so that the prices would drop. As a result the factories stood still for many months, innovation slowed down and some businesses went bankrupt.

The second pillar revolves around competitive industries, which means to build European industrial leadership with dedicated support for ICT, nanotechnology, biotechnology and photonics – so called "Key Enabling Technologies." Development of these technologies requires a multi-disciplinary knowledge and capital intensive approach. It means to ensure that whatever is invented in a laboratory is put to use in a factory. European private businesses find themselves reluctant to invest in R&D – how to value and valorise knowledge is quite a difficult thing for them. As stated before, it is not the creation of knowledge which is a European weakness, but the capacity to make money from knowledge is. The second pillar is designed to ameliorate this.

Third, there is the pillar of "Better Society." Main aim here is to bring research and knowledge to concrete innovation in the lives of citizens,[75] focusing on the following six topics:

1. Health, demographic change and wellbeing
2. Food security, sustainable agriculture, marine and maritime research and the bio-economy
3. Secure, clean and efficient energy challenge[76]
4. Smart, green and integrated transport challenge[77]
5. Climate action, resource efficiency and raw materials
6. Inclusive, innovative and secure societies

Having covered the EU2020 and Horizon2020, we can return to the main question of this paper: What does it take to bring innovation in European business to a higher level, making it more competitive on a global scale, and what can be learned from a comparison with the United States?

## 3. Comparison of entrepreneurial culture between Europe and the United States

Innovation means to bring new products to the market – there are 500 million Europeans, which is a very large market. How interesting this is becomes clear by casting a glance at the United States´ innovation: If you look at the past ten years, what the United States invested in BRICS was only 7% of what it invested in Europe. The GDP is higher than that of China or the United States. An American and a European researcher have the same starting point. Both come from university, make a discovery, and consequently search for a way to transmute this discovery into a

---

[75] The FP7 is mainly oriented at the needs of ELS rather than the needs of society. Thus it is relevant to emphasize that III is *not* a cooperation pillar of FP7.

[76] The reports from the Horizon2020 thematic workshops can be found at: http://ec.europa.eu/research/horizon2020/index_en.cfm?pg=workshops&workshop=smart_green_integrated_transport

[77] Ibid

business. In the United States, the researcher will usually come equipped with some knowledge on legal matters and access to funding. The European one will need to speak to a lawyer, and most of the time he will not even understand what the lawyer is telling him. In Europe corporate life is more entrenched and regulated, and less permeable to outsiders. What we lack is a network of knowledge that surrounds the entrepreneur. This is what we need to set up.

Europe's bankruptcy laws make an entrepreneurial endeavour seem like madness – one is essentially given only a single chance. Some Member States hold one accountable for about 4-5 years after a bankruptcy declaration has been completed. Compare this to one year accountability in the United States. In this regard product innovation is left to already established companies, ones that could take the risk and pay it off if it doesn't work out. Securing a bank loan as a form of business capital (once again as a non-established player) is a route not widely pursued by many as it comes with massive waiting times and yet again more red tape.

Being a European, the environment generally does not support an individual in bringing his idea forward and translating it into an enterprise. First one will need consultancy, which means speaking to a lawyer, which in turn means that one requires money. Then, after these consultation processes, at the end of the day, the person will make up the balance and realize that it's just not worth it for the reason that it is too complicated to actually set the business up. This is the scenario for young people with an entrepreneurial spirit in Europe today. In the United States, by contrast, initiatives such as *quickstarter* flourish. This is a website where entrepreneurs can post their ideas – investors can easily select initiatives they wish to support. What is necessary is a closer involvement of business in high education sectors. Education, in Europe, is more of a public entity with a public mission.

In other words, the common route is usually:

School → University → Employment

Rather than:

School → University → Taking a risk – simply because the risk turns out to be too great.

In the United States´ National Science Foundation, scientists decide which projects are funding-worthy. In 2012, Obama requested funding of $7.373 billion for the fiscal year 2013. The National Science Board is a President appointed, senate confirmed body of governors who meet six times a year to set out the overall agenda but the day to day running is done by fellow scientists. It is much less political than Europe which has competing national agencies, and a reputation for funding research of political friends. Meaning that every Member States wants to champion its own university. This is navel-gazing, and one day one looks up and sees China conquering space. Competence and brilliance are not only in Germany – they might be in Poland and Estonia, which means that resources must be able to spill over.

Summarizing this, the culture in Europe may change over time, but not immediately. To contribute to this end, we must create the right preconditions for innovation. Companies must do the bulk of the innovation themselves but can benefit from the European Investment Bank. Governments must present the view that businesses are welcome as long as they conform to the European guidelines. Rules should be simple so that companies have enough manoeuvring space. A closer involvement of business in high education sectors is necessary as well.

## 4. Suggestions to bolster competitiveness on a European level

The European Patent is also important. There must be a stimulus to keep innovating – in other words to eliminate the danger that three months later a Chinese company is copying your invention very cheaply because their personnel is literally working for a few bags of rice. Whoever invests in R&D must be able to reap the rewards of that. In this context it is important to emphasize the importance of the European Patent. Whoever wants a patent currently has to request this in each separate Member State and translate this to all languages. If it is breached, one has to go to court in each State, as well. The European Court that will deal with the upcoming European Patent is being divided over three separate Member States. Even if the European Patent will not solve all problems, it will certainly protect innovation without a delay of months to translate an idea into 23 languages. Even if some Member States are reluctant to join at this point in time, they likely will at a later stage.

When it comes to innovation, the key to success is to present a good quality product for low prices. Unifying the market and removing unnecessary costs has certainly benefited business; arguably, however, this has not bolstered innovation.

All products and services must fall under the same European legislation. This will bring benefits of scale as well as increased oversight. Monitoring and supervising the market will become easier, as well. In the present situation, to eliminate the risk of a spontaneous flame in your pocket, European lighters must be pressed so hard that one's thumb starts to hurt. Right now, we have cheap Chinese lighters flooding the market through the harbour of Rotterdam. This is bad news for a Member State like Bulgaria. The supervision is poor and the consumer has no awareness of European safety standards. As a result, 10.000 European workers lose their jobs, and the companies that have adjusted their lighters to the safety standards are punished. These kinds of situations are under-illuminated and illustrate that there is a lot to gain from improving the market conditions without having to turn on the tap of subsidies.

At a certain point, if everything the consumer buys has "made in China" written all over it, people will lose interest. The consumer has a perception of quality; Italian fashion, German *gründlichkeit*, cars, French wine . . . If, however, on a shirt, the last button is made in Italy, then a company has the right to say: "Made in Italy." The factories concerned have been outsourced, because in Bangladesh people don't give as much heed to legislation concerning, for instance, work involving chemicals. But what we *can* do is to bring these industries back to Europe. A *good governance mindset* among the consumers would be beneficial to this.

In response to globalisation we need to reflect upon the question: "How are we going to re-launch industry in Europe?" The answer to this question will be with preparation for the future as well as the solution to the current crisis. With a rising global population, comes a rising demand for industrial products. The current debt-crisis and the solvency issues it comes with unfortunately make this solution difficult to accomplish, as a part of the incentive for business to do this will need to come from the government. The state-age-framework ensures there is fair competition between 27 Member States. Legal constraints determine that a state cannot give more than a certain percentage of support. Therefore, the state-age-framework serves as an obstacle to re-industrializing Europe, which is not adjusted to the global age. The Obama administration, by contrast, made it a clear point of policy that any American enterprise ready to source back to the United States will be supported in doing so.

At this point we must emphasize the importance of *reciprocity*. When it comes to public expenditure, the European Union is not protectionist, which is to keep things competitive. The United States, by contrast, made it a matter of law that at least 50% of the airline stock shares must be in American hands. Also the expenditure of large projects go to small sized domestic companies. Reciprocity is important because one does not want some global power to flood your market with their products, while buying none of yours in return. Thus, we must be willing to open up the European market for foreign goods and services, but only if those foreign powers, in return, also open up to ours. Without reciprocity, a state like China can hoard money and have a high quantity of production due to low costs of labour and low standards of living. This will destabilize the global market to the disadvantage of European enterprise. Some Members of European Parliament, like Morten Løkkegaard, are opposed to reciprocity since they fear a Chinese trade boycott. The Chinese, however, need to sell their stuff somewhere, which means either Europe or the United States, and thus a trade embargo is not a realistic scenario.

## 5. The re-industrialisation of Europe

Some liberals might, at first glance, be sceptical about the suggestion of re-launching industry in Europe; it would require government interference in the economy.

The problem is that for people reasoning in this way, a *sense of historic momentum* is lacking. In the first paragraph we have concluded that the European Union is the market leader of the world. The twenty years that we find ourselves facing will determine whether Europe can be one of the three global world players next to the United States and China, or if we choose to enter the periphery of geopolitics – allow ourselves to seep quietly into the darkness after leaving so much of our science and culture to world history. It really comes down to people with a degree of influence reading a paper like this and realizing, *truly understanding*, what is at stake. And this is hard in an age where the elites find themselves surrounded by so much prosperity that they take it for granted.

I recently heard an anecdote of a person working at the Berlaymont who once sat next to an important Chinese diplomat. He conveyed his grief to the Chinese official for losing over what he estimated to be forty-six thousand soldiers in the Chinese-Vietnam war of 1979. "Forty-six thousand?" the official replied, "That is just the growth of the Chinese population within one hour. For the last 2200 years, the Chinese economy has, on average, been the largest economy of the world. With an exception for the last two hundred years. For this century, we plan to bridge that gap."

Even for those who find relief in choosing to think the exact figures of this anecdote are slightly exaggerated, the sense of historic momentum should be clear. Another example is Africa: in 1950 there were about 230 million people living on the African continent. By 2050, this will have multiplied to 2,2 billion human beings, even becoming 3,5 billion by the end of this century. By itself, Nigeria will have a populace of 440 million by 2050, greater than for example the United States.[78] What we are dealing with here, when speaking about the rise of BRICS, is a transformation of global world power. The world population is growing, and thus these new consumers will demand products. Whoever has the industrial capacity to supply these products will rule the world.

China has hoarded up money through selling products created by low-wage salaries and has used this money to buy up United States bonds. This means that the United States´ economic stability is in Chinese hands, and whenever an American somewhere around the world lives in a house that is two sizes too big for him, it is because a Chinese citizen pays for that. And they are willing to pay for that because they know this will fortify the political position of their nation in the long run, and have a strong sense of nationalism. This nationalism manifests itself economically, as China has set up the largest investment funds in the world that buys up natural resources, 90% of which are at present controlled by the Chinese state. [79]

---

[78] United Nations, *Department of Economic and Social Affairs, World Populations Prospects: 2012 revision*, 2013. http://www.pewresearch.org/fact-tank/2014/02/03/10-projections-for-the-global-population-in-2050/

[79] "China presently produces over 95% of all rare earth materials that are vital in creating various electronic technologies including lithium car batteries, solar panels, wind turbines, flat-screen television, compact fluorescent light bulbs, petroleum-to-gasoline catalytic cracking, and military defense components including missile guidance systems. It also dominates abilities to process them. This enables it to attract product manufactures to operate there as a condition of doing business, ration exports to maximize prices, and punish nations that don't go along with its policy interests through supply embargoes." Source: http://www.forbes.com/sites/larrybell/2012/04/15/chinas-rare-earth-metals-

A service-based economy, like we have in Europe, is bound to collapse in circumstances like these. What ultimately constitutes the standards of living for a human life? Products and the resources that these products are created from. Not services or currencies – these will rapidly lose value once resources become sufficiently scarce, and they will become scarce as long as the world population continues to grow. China realizes this, which explains their economic nationalism and their preparedness to invest large amounts of finances into securing raw natural resources. The answer that Europe needs to give to this geopolitical shift, is to either adopt the same sort of economic neo-colonialism, or to invest resources into creating artificial resource materials that can replace the natural ones. This will require large scale investment in laboratories and industrial production facilities. Hence the re-industrialisation of Europe is necessary. We will be able to profile our products as "EU quality level," and in doing so become an appealing option for world citizen consumers. The alternative is accepting that China will dominate the world.

At the end of the day, Chinese economic nationalism counts on European laissez-faire liberalism to be blinded by its momentary prosperity and not waking up in time and doing what is necessary. It takes visionaries and philosophers to speak up about this.

## 6. Liberal values in an age of economic globalism

From the days of Adam Smith to Bismarck even to today, a large share of liberalism's appeal is in creating a single market through the elimination of tariffs and guild regulations. Eventually, Europeans might find out that they need to intertwine their economies and move together as a power bloc. However the breaking down of these barriers, as pointed out previously, is going

---

monopoly-neednt-put-an-electronics-stranglehold-on-america/ (4/15/2012) The author notes that Beijing reduced rare earth shipments by 9% in 2010 and has recently announced plans to reduce exports by another 35%.

too slowly. At the end of the day, no Member State is inclined to give up sovereignty, but what they *do* want, is to make money.

As Guy Verhofstadt once said, it is better to pool sovereignty than to lose it in globalisation. Let us hark back to the shifting geopolitical economic order I pointed out in the first section. We live in an age of globalisation, and right now Europe is a service-based economy. Typical for the age of globalisation the majority of people work in services, whereas the majority of the European population worked in agriculture only 40 years ago. Agriculture is becoming an industry if this isn't already the case in most Member States. A service-based economy can thrive as long as there is a stable, world-leading currency and as long as the resources are imported from elsewhere to maintain the standards of living. Western citizens have a large global footprint, since they consume many materials that are transported from abroad.

The earth's population of human beings is still rising, and Western enterprises consider it as in their interests to develop foreign indigenous peoples into new bourgeoisies. This is to increase the amount of consumers and market available to them to cater their goods and services. What is, however, not taken into account is that this development means a huge drain upon the resources of the earth. With a higher standard of living comes a higher demand for the processing of natural resources. This claim ultimately transforms into a political claim at a transnational level.

This effectively means that service-based economies will either collapse in the near future, or will be forced to make large compromises to their standards of living. Even if service-based economies can dominate financial markets with their currencies, then still no power will be prepared to accept amounts of digitally created money as a trade for the real, tangible natural resources people require in life on a daily basis. Thus, for example, we know that although China owns most of the United States through bonds and stock shares on paper, the United States will never allow the Chinese government to transmute these financial claims into claims upon property in terms of companies and resources, and to move these away from the American soil. This would leave the citizens destitute and no government will accept that.

Complicating this issue even further is the capitalistic nature of globalism. Capitalism is not a set of moral values but rather a mindset aimed at the productivity of output. Even strong laissez-faire liberals would agree that the process of capitalism requires some regulation – for instance to prevent the rise of monopolies that will transform into oligarchies, ultimately using their unique access to scarce resources and necessary products to impose political rules. After all, capitalism is a process towards profit optimization and will not conform to moral values unless these are imposed from a greater power the markets find in their way. Usually this process does not meet much resistance since moral values are imbedded within the social fabric of the society in which commercial enterprise operates. However such universal moral standards are missing when we deal with this issue at a geopolitical level. For example standards of human rights are not necessarily acceptable to powers in Asia or the Middle East. There is not a real power to impose these standards, and if there were, this power, as well as the standards it imposes, would perpetually be contested.

This conflict of short term (profit from a wider consumer base through development of a global bourgeois) and long term (resource scarcity) interests seems commercially too painful and eth(n)ically too politically sensitive to address. Yet it is something that will need to be addressed – and needs to be at the heart of foreign as well as industrial policy – if Europe is not to go down under in a globalizing world. Underlying this picture is a widely shared worldview that stems from the late nineteenth century and was by held positivists, anarchists and socialists alike. Philosophers like Rousseau, Comte, Marx and Kropotkin have held this view, which can be characterized as a deep belief that all human beings are in essence equal since all human beings have the same biological bodily needs.

From this follows the assumption that man is malleable, and will adapt to any social circumstance as it arises. All humans share fundamental wants such as sufficient food to fill their grumbling stomachs and a peaceful environment for their children to grow up in. These fundamental needs will lead the peoples of earth to realize they can build a better world by working together, and in the future the cultural and spiritual differences which are the causes of conflicts will no longer exist. In the positivist mindset all conflicts are the results of scarcity, and by working together as brothers and sharing the scientific research, technology will provide the abundance that will make scarcity obsolete. Not crime, but poverty will be outlawed, since crime and war stem from the need and envy that are by-products of inequality. This frame of mind is backed by the Maslow pyramid, meaning that all populations ultimately strive for self-actualization. Once they become sufficiently developed the populaces would inevitably throw off the shackles of restrictive religions and repressive regimes. At the end of the day, thus it is assumed, theocratic and collectivist totalitarian doctrines and regimes would lose their capacity to motivate people in a world where the common standards of living are sufficiently developed.

This view, however, although widely spread, is deeply historicist, as it counts on the beneficial results of scientific research which has not yet been executed. Who is to say whether the resources to conduct this future research will even be available, as the commercial use of resources is obviously more lucrative on the short term, while the markets continue to pull? Regardless of our more or less equal bodily needs, our characters and the cultures we are brought up in decide how we will interact with the environment. How intelligent and passionate to find solutions one is, ultimately decides the kind of solutions one will come up with. Whether one will invest an hour each day to bring a bucket of water to water the crops, or will dig a ditch to provide irrigation for the rest of a lifetime.

Culture is a major force in shaping both economic circumstances as well as individual characters. The 'tabula rasa' mindset of the common positivist worldview is utterly naive if not downright incorrect. Westerners tend to expect the globalisation to funnel a mixture of universal human rights, multiculturalism and consumerism all over the world. This is what happened to Western society – yet Western society is thus far the only civilization to reach the post-industrial stage. We see that civic freedoms have declined in nations such as Turkey and Russia while wealth and consumerism increased simultaneously. The Indonesian province Atjeh has recently adopted Sharia law, as have several provinces of Nigeria.[80]

As a result of the described shifts in economy and population, the global power structure will change. Power will shift towards those who have access to natural resources and possess the industrial capacity to process them. We already see Chinese companies emerging in places like Africa, Suriname and even Greenland. Mining operations are starting everywhere, and should the global temperature increase so that the natural resources of Greenland become accessible, all this will be gone within short notice. The bottom line of all this is that the Western world, and Europe in particular, needs a new story for a new generation. Not a story about exploitation, but about the good things that Europe has left to the world in regards of science and culture. We must grow beyond that which the German philosopher Friedrich Nietzsche would describe as a guilt-complex rooted within our Christian history, and accept that it is not a bad thing if Western civilization is dominant on earth. The alternative is not a bright scenario for the sustainability of the world.

In Europe, there is a political culture of cutting away from the top and adding this to close up gaps in the bottom. Through our 'levelling' we tend towards egalitarianism. The whole system of the United States, by contrast, is built to benefit the best, the top-performing. As a result they stimulate competition and new initiatives. Going by the American position, the most widely shared European views on economy and society stimulate laziness.

---

[80] Sharia has been instituted as civil and criminal law in 9 Muslim-majority and parts of 3 Muslim-plurality states since 1999, when Zamfara State governor Ahmad Rufai Sani began the push for the institution of Sharia at state level of government. Source: http://news.bbc.co.uk/2/hi/africa/1885052.stm

As already concluded, we need to re-industrialize Europe. Government involvement is required for this, yet the concept of handing out grants is not very liberal. We consider this to be up to the bank and business sectors. But here in Europe we have a different culture than in the United States. Everyone waits for the government to invest in research. What we need is money to support the risk investment, because this will make banks more inclined to support these forms of research. Equity financing means to support venture capital investors to cover a part of the risk they are taking by investing in companies; a joint equity financing instrument. It is generally easier to convince a French company to rely on equity financing than a German one. As previously mentioned, the European Investment Bank could help out in this, and provide a guarantee to private investment. If a company supports a research project, the bank could cover potential losses. This is an RSI: a Risk Sharing Instrument launched by European Investment Funds. Investments in small, risky projects will become attractive. As a liberal, one holds that the state should not be burdened with investigating the risks of particular entrepreneurial projects – thus, instead, the legislation should be simplified to give way to venture capital.

## 7. Conclusion

At the end of the day, Europe may have a larger base of consumers, but lacks the scale advantage that the United States has. The European decentralisation makes it too hard to bundle the efforts. This can be fixed through things such as a European Patent, Horizon2020 investments in improving the digital infrastructure, enhancing researcher mobility, stimulating banks to fund R&D projects while backing the risks, and the termination of loads of "red tape" bureaucracy. A deeper symbiosis between profit-oriented private business and education with a public mission is also beneficial. Ultimately, what we require is a re-industrialized Europe; because in the global age of overpopulation and rising demands, power will drift to those who have the capacity for mining and refining natural resources, and processing them efficiently into consumer goods.

When making business deals with powers outside of Europe, an amount of reciprocity in trade must be observed. Geopolitical considerations make clear that complete liberal laissez-faire ideology is ultimately not feasible: Industrial and political power will need to converge to obtain and safeguard those natural resources which are necessary to secure a decent standard of living in the long run. It is imperative that Europeans can continue to set the global standards for matters of product and food quality.

Since China owns an increasing share of raw natural resources, we have to ask ourselves if we can fabricate materials to replace these. For this, it would be beneficial to work together with the United States. Those who work today to find solutions to these questions will be the world leaders of tomorrow. Although whether a specific "who" or "what" can be identified as a world leader is, in the age of globalisation, not so clear anymore.

# TOINE SCHOUTETEN
## Opening up the Union: the Increase of EU-Connectivity by Railroad

*"The one moral, the one remedy for every evil, social, political, financial, and industrial, the one immediate vital need of the entire Republic, is the Transcontinental Railroad."*
Rocky Mountain News, 1866

### Introduction

On May 10th 1869, three years after the publication of the above-mentioned statement, the Transcontinental Railroad was finished. As a consequence of this ingenuous piece of work, the United States thrived in ways that had never been imagined before: the railroad was a key element in the transition from an agrarian to an industrial society, in the settling of the continent, and in the rise of wage labour[81][82][83].

Nowadays, within the European Union, the need for constructing such grand, physical structures is less pressing: over 212.500 km of railway lines connect most of the continent and its 500 million citizens, only leaving the connectivity of the new Member States to be desired[84]. In comparison, the USA nowadays employs 140.000 miles or about 225.000 km of railroads[85].

---

[81] White, R. *Railroaded: The Transcontinentals and the Making of Modern America*, 2010. W. W. Norton & Company.
[82] Review of *Railroaded* by Scott Martelle. http://www.washingtonpost.com/entertainment/books/richard-whites-railroaded-the-transcontinentals-and-the-making-of-modern-america/2011/04/04/gIQAvBKzwI_story.html?wprss=
[83] *The Impact of the Transcontinental Railroad.* http://www.pbs.org/wgbh/americanexperience/features/general-article/tcrr-impact/
[84] Facts and figures about the EU railway network. http://ec.europa.eu/transport/strategies/facts-and-figures/all-themes/index_en.htm
[85] Facts and figures about the USA railway network. https://www.aar.org/todays-railroads/our-network

However, the EU does face various apparent and less-apparent challenges: at the forefront, the media are flooded with internal cases of disparities, such as the issues regarding the repayment of Greek debt, as well as cases of disparities in which bordering nations are involved, such as the crisis in Ukraine and the interweaved involvement of Russia. In the background, a gap is growing between southern and northern EU Member States based on differences in financial mentality and the resulting financial systems[86] [87], whilst it appears that euro-scepticism is the only thing that unites EU citizens[88].

At this point, I refer to the statement mentioned at the start of this paper and the historic process on which it is based: it shows that railroads can offer both a literal and figurative way of dealing with widespread challenges and problems.

In this paper, I want to showcase that one of many solutions to counter the EU-challenges is to build a structure *via* the European railroads. By building, I do not mean forging steel and melting iron, but by making travelling by track less complicated for the future of Europe. In other words: to pave the way, rocks need not to be crushed and the landscape needs not to be smoothed, but instead the bar for the European youth to voyage by rail needs to be lowered. Indeed, the Union needs to be opened up by opening up the railroads.

In the remainder of this paper, I will provide a short overview of the current situation on the railroads within the EU and the possibilities and impossibilities that are intertwined with this situation. Alongside this, I will portray several ways in which these possibilities can be utilized and how the impossibilities can be

---

[86] *Europe's Two Speed Economy: North vs South.* http://economix.blogs.nytimes.com/2010/07/28/europes-two-speed-economy-north-vs-south/?_r=0

[87] *Southern European workers vs Northern European Workers.* https://rwer.wordpress.com/2011/10/24/southern-european-workers-versus-northern-european-workers-5-charts/

[88] *Anti-EU, Far-Right Parties Post Strong Gains in European Elections.* http://www.wsj.com/articles/SB10001424052702304811904579585732459776154

nullified. Finally, a short conclusion has been included at the end of this paper.

# 1
## The Present State of the Union

At the time of writing this report, several discount programmes are in effect. Some examples are the Benelux Pass, which offers the traveller a number of days to travel within one month, the Scandinavia pass, with which one can travel for a fixed amount of days within two months, and the Eurail Global Pass, which offers the traveller either a fixed amount of days to travel within a period or a period in which one can travel unlimited[89]. It is self-evident that the option last mentioned is considerably more expensive.

Two issues immediately come to one's attention when reading the specifications of these programmes: they are rather expensive, even when a discount is included, and usually they are only worth one's while when a trip of several weeks or longer is undertaken or when one is planning to stay for several days or even weeks at the destination. It is reasonable to assume that the neutralisation of said issues would stimulate youngsters to travel more by train or to travel by train at all.

The institution to which the task of synchronising the European railway system has been delegated, is the European Railway Agency (ERA) [90]. A vast majority of ERA's goals focus on issues regarding safety standards and information exchange. Of course, these issues are of a vital importance in synchronising the European railway system, but they do not deal with the interests of the European travellers that are under investigation in this report. This fact provides another reason why a EU wide programme should be implemented, in order to take away the barriers that international travellers are confronted with.

The future of the European railway system provides another reason why the implementation of the options, described in the

---

[89] Railway Fares for the Youth in Europe. http://www.raileurope-world.com/special-offers/discounted-fares/article/youth-fares

[90] European Railway Agency Facts & Figures. http://www.era.europa.eu/The-Agency/About-ERA/Pages/Home.aspx

next section of this paper, should be implemented[91]. Because of intensifying competition within the railroad industry, customer focus of the operators will increase. However, on cross-border routes, no one operator will own the customer: they will need to learn how to share.

Next to this, cooperation will extend across borders: not just national frontiers, but commercial, industrial and organisational borders too. Travellers do not see these borders, they are only focussed on their destination.

## 2
## Paving the Way

As I have described in the previous section, the flexibility and costs of EU wide options to travel by train need to be tackled. The current objectives of ERA, which is the pre-eminent institution for integrating the European railway system, do not, however, deal with these issues. Next to this, the expectations regarding the future of the European railway system show that an answer is desired and perhaps even needed.

In my opinion, it is first demand of transport by train which needs to be adjusted, after which supply can be created. This poses less of a risk for public institutions, because it is far less costly to adjust or terminate an EU-wide funding programme of train tickets for youngsters than it is to undo the changes made to tracks, trains, workforce and/or the railway operators in general. The latter should be adapted, for that matter, sooner or later, considering the numerous instances of inefficient and ineffective cross-border rail links[92]. This is, however, out of the scope for this paper.

In adjusting demand, I would like to propose two options: the Dutch system and the Belgian system. It is important to note that these are not mutually exclusive options. Rather, a combination of the two systems would perhaps be most favourable, but is out of

---

[91] *The Rail Journey to 2020.* http://www.amadeusrail.net/white-papers
[92] *Cross Border Rail Links in Europe.* http://www.hiddeneurope.co.uk/cross-border-rail-links-in-europe

the reach of the matters dealt with in this paper. I did, however, take the liberty to describe some minor cross-overs.

# 3
# The Dutch System

In the Netherlands, every student who is entitled to a Dutch student loan, is also entitled to a so called student OV-card[93]. This entitlement can be used to obtain either a week product or a weekend product.

A week product allows a student to travel for free by public transportation from Monday 4.00AM until Saturday 4.00AM. During the remaining hours, travelling is possible by buying regular tickets at a 40% discount.

A weekend product allows a student to travel for free by public transportation from Friday 12.00PM until Monday 4.00AM. During the remainder of the week, students can travel by buying regular tickets at a 40% discount[94].

As can be found on the website of DUO, which is the Dutch institution for all student related matters, the entitlement to a student OV-card is part of a student loan which is provided by the Dutch government. The student OV-card is therefore not free at all, unless a Bachelor's degree or a Master's degree is obtained: in that case, the loan is turned into a grant.

The description of the Dutch system for students to travel by public transportation shows a number of details and complications, which need to be dealt with in order to make this system appropriate for the EU as a whole.

Firstly, one has to be entitled to a student loan. In an EU context, this could be interpreted as being part of the Erasmus programme. However, this leaves out a vast majority of the European youth that

---

[93] Specifications student travel product in the Netherlands. http://duo.nl/particulieren/international-student/student-travel-product/collecting-your-student-travel-product.asp

[94] Overview free travelling & discounted travelling for students in the Netherlands. https://duo.nl/particulieren/student-hbo-of-universiteit/ov-en-reizen/wanneer-reizen-in-week-en-weekend.asp

is not a part of the Erasmus programme. It is for this reason that I think that one of the features of the Belgian system should be incorporated by the implementation of this system: all people up until a certain age, e.g. the age of 25, are entitled to make use of the programme.

Secondly, a one to one implementation of the Dutch system, by allowing the European youth to travel for free or a discount during all days, would cause an excessive burden on both the EU and the public transportation operators. The first would have to fund a programme of monstrous proportions, whilst some young Europeans will use it at a minimal level or even not at all; the latter would have to implement a much more flexible structure and a much bigger capacity to deal with sudden flows of European youngsters. In order to deal with these drawbacks, several options are possible.
The first remedy provides every European young citizen with an option to register his preferences for the periods of time in which he or she would like to make use of the EU railway programme. In case some periods of time are overbooked, a lottery can be used to assign the subscribers to these popular periods of time. The second remedy consists of indeed providing an all year round programme, but at a much lower discount than is the case in the Netherlands at this very moment.

The viability of the countermeasures mentioned above need, of course, to be investigated further in order to ensure that this system is as successful as it could be.

Finally, the funds to turn this programme into reality need to be created or subtracted from other sources. In my opinion, the programme should be connected with education: European teenagers and adolescents that decide to take part in any of the EU accredited forms of education should be able to make use of a programme in which they can experience what people, cultures and life in general is like in other parts of the Union. Thereby, the EU can kill two birds with one stone: Europe's next generation is both educated and culturally literate.

# 4
# The Belgian System

In Belgium, all people under the age of 26, whether they are students or not, can buy a Go Pass. This pass offers its user a single journey to any destination in Belgium for a fixed price of €6 on any day during the week[95].

Next to this, it is possible to buy a Go Pass for 10 trips within Belgium for a mere €50[96]. Again, the traveller has to be under the age of 26, the pass can be used on any day during the week, and it can be shared by several passengers.

As is the case with the Dutch System, implementing the Belgian System one-to-one on an EU-wide scale could cause several severe drawbacks.

The basic Go Pass is in essence very much comparable to the programmes that are available at this moment, such as the Eurail Pass: a discount is offered to citizens up until a certain age. However, in comparing these two kinds of programmes, a major issue arises. The Belgian Go Pass offers much more flexibility by allowing the passenger to travel to any destination on any day for a fixed price. The Eurail Pass on the other hand does not offer this much flexibility, as I have described in the previous sections. It is for this reason that the idea behind the Go Pass is preferable: it offers flexibility to its users, which might indeed open up the railways for the youth of Europe.

For the 10 Fare Go Pass, it is possible to share the right to travel with several passengers. In an EU perspective, this would cause avoidable fraud-risks: the EU right to travel, if it is to be shareable, could be used by several ineligible citizens. It is for this reason that I propose that the programme is to be person-specific; sharing of the travel-document, and thereby the right to travel, is not allowed.

---

[95] Belgian Railway Services: Go Pass. http://www.belgianrail.be/en/travel-tickets/tickets/~/media/1C727ED3F68747C49A8864C6435A1920.ashx

[96] Belgian Railway Services: 10 fare Go Pass. http://www.visitbelgium.com/?page=transportation

In finishing up the analysis of both the Dutch and the Belgian systems, both offer major opportunities in opening up the possibilities for the European youth to explore everything that the EU and its member-states have to offer. Of course, these systems cannot be copied on a European level; they need to be tailored and perhaps even combined in order to become a valuable part of everything that the EU has to offer.

## Conclusion

In the course of this paper, I depicted the current and future situation on the EU railroads and I mentioned several aspects of this situation that could be improved. Alongside this, I offered two options in which the metaphorical barriers for young Europeans to travel by train can be overcome. Once again, I want to point out that these are not mutually exclusive options. Rather, a combination of the two systems would perhaps be the best option available, but it is not within the scope of the matters dealt with in this paper.

By realising that youth is indeed the future of the EU and, as a consequence, that youth is key in diminishing regional disparities over time, one could very well say that by opening up the railroads and thereby opening up opportunities to get to know other people, countries and cultures, the EU can open up as a whole and the Union might thrive in ways that have never been imagined before.

I do realise that the propositions made in this paper are no quick fixes, nor are they to be implemented point-to-point. However, I firmly believe that a fundamental improvement of the wellbeing of all EU citizens and the Union as a whole should be achieved by a bold mixture of short-term and long-term measures, one of which could be based on the idea and a mixture of the policies proposed in this paper.

www.ingramcontent.com/pod-product-compliance
Lightning Source LLC
Chambersburg PA
CBHW060903170526
45158CB00001B/480